武

THE WAY OF THE SPIRITUAL WARRIOR

士

道

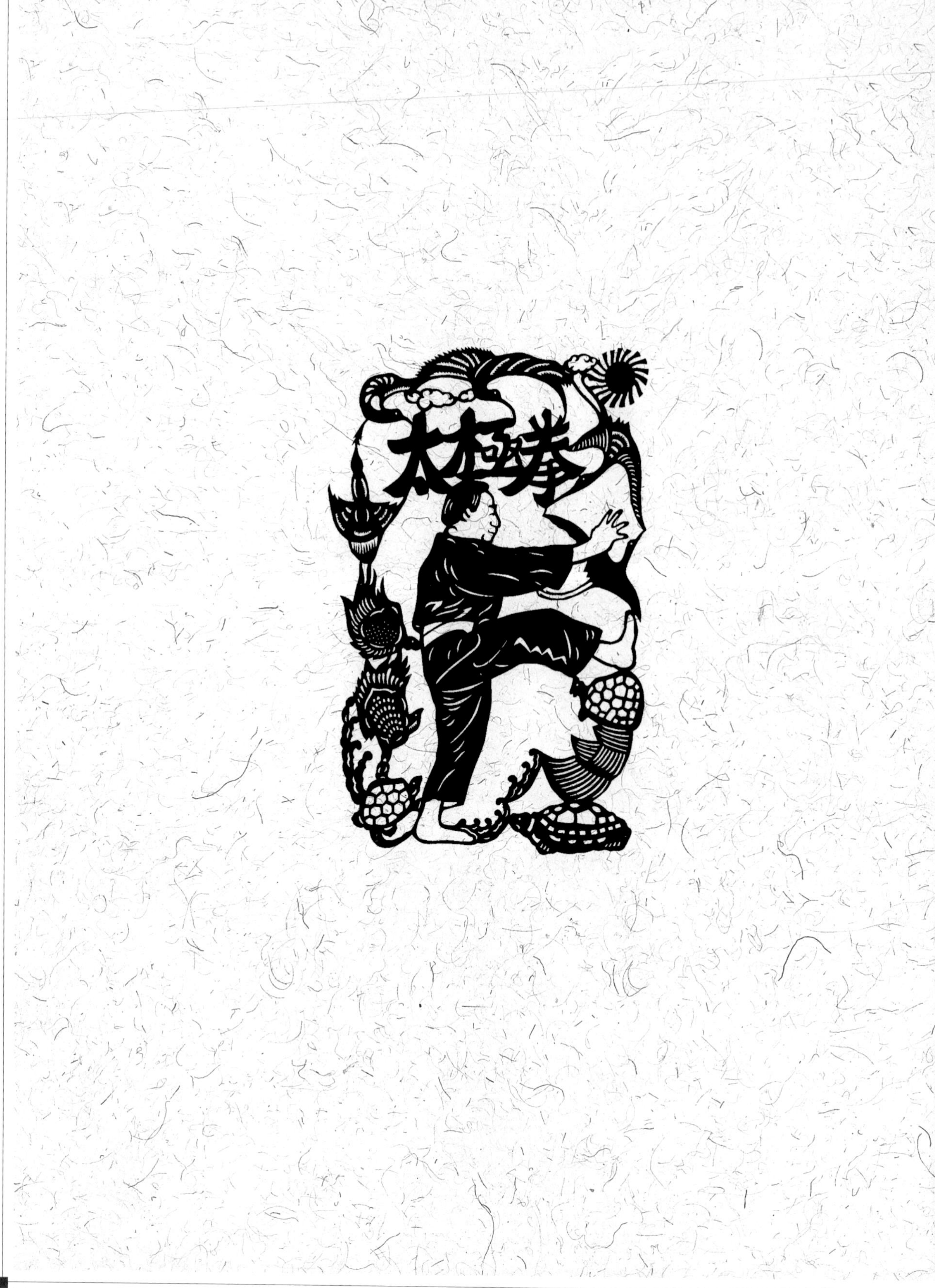
太極拳

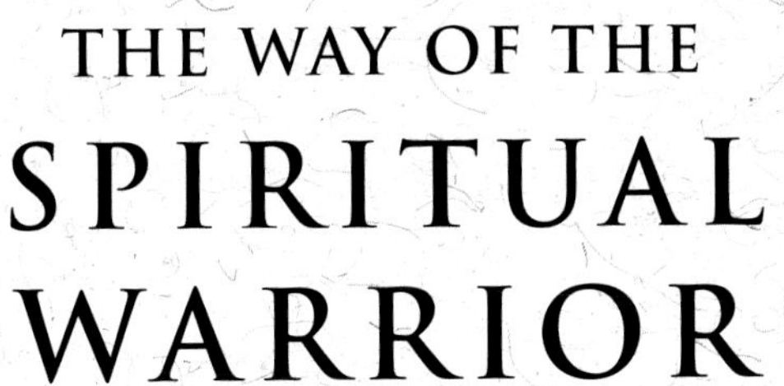

THE WAY OF THE SPIRITUAL WARRIOR

IMPROVING MIND, BODY, AND SPIRIT WITH THE SOFT MARTIAL-ARTS STYLE

PAUL BRECHER

Thorsons
An Imprint of HarperCollins*Publishers*

THIS BOOK IS DEDICATED TO
THE BRAVEST WARRIOR, MY SON JED

Thorsons
An imprint of HarperCollins *Publishers*
77–85 Fulham Palace Road
Hammersmith, London W6 8JB

Published in the UK by Thorsons 1998
1 3 5 7 9 10 8 6 4 2

Produced for Thorsons
by Godsfield Press
Designed and edited by
The Bridgewater Book CompanyLtd.

Picture research *Jane Moore and Vanessa Fletcher*
Illustrations *Michael Courteney, Lorraine Harrison, Ivan Hissey, Andrew Kulman and Sarah Young*
Studio Photography *Silvio Dokov and Guy Ryecart*
Calligraphy *Tai Bo Ling*

Paul Brecher asserts the moral right to be identified as the author of this work

A catalogue record for this book is available from the British Library.

ISBN 07225 3743 3

Printed in Hong Kong

Neither the publisher nor author can be held responsible for injury sustained while practicing techniques shown in this book. This book is for reference purposes only and should persons choose to study Chi Kung, or any other soft internal martial arts styles described in this book, they should do so under the guidance of a qualified instructor.

Contents

Introduction

THIS BOOK IS an introduction to the internal martial arts. It aims to explain the history, philosophy, and practice of the internal styles, and to show how they can help in the development of body, mind, and spirit.

The internal styles are all primarily based on the practice of forms - a series of self-defense movements - such as punches, kicks, and palm strikes that are practiced one after the other in a pre-arranged flowing way, in the same way that a dancer links together a series of turns and steps to create a choreographed dance sequence. Although every movement has a self-defense application, the forms are more than just a martial art: they are a healing art in that they teach ways of developing better physical, mental, and emotional balance and stability.

The soft internal martial arts such as Taijiquan concentrate on the body's internal energy.

The hard martial arts, such as Kung Fu, concentrate on developing muscle power in the limbs.

There are several different internal styles, each with their own forms, but common to them all is that they are done without any unnecessary muscle tension that might restrict the flow of internal energy. This is the reason why the internal martial arts styles are also called soft styles.

The internal (soft) martial arts differ from the external (hard) martial arts in many ways (see page 11). In general though, hard styles, such as Karate and Shaolin Kung Fu, use linear movements that require muscle tension and place more emphasis on the development of the muscle power in the local limbs. The soft styles are more circular and

flowing, requiring virtually no muscle tension at all and placing more emphasis on the development of internal energy throughout the whole body. This energy is called Qi by the Chinese and Ki by the Japanese. When cultivated properly, it not only adds power to self-defense techniques, but also aids in the development of good health, a sense of well-being, and the ability to touch upon one's true spiritual nature. A strong Qi flow creates a clear and calm mind, a strong spirit, and great longevity. Qi is a universal energy that flows through all living things. By training in the internal styles of the martial arts, we can not only improve our own health by increasing our Qi, but also, when practicing the styles at a high level, we can use our Qi to heal others.

This book explains with equal measure both the martial and healing aspects of the internal martial arts: not to give them equal emphasis would lead to an unbalanced training program. The forms of the internal martial arts are not just a way practicing punches and kicks, they are also a type of moving meditation for developing and improving body, mind, and spirit (see page 13).

Chapter 1 examines the core principles of the internal martial arts from the techniques to the philosophy that are common to all of the styles; the differences between internal and external styles; the philosophy underpinning the internal styles; how the forms can be used as a type of moving meditation for spiritual development; how to strengthen the will through training; and how

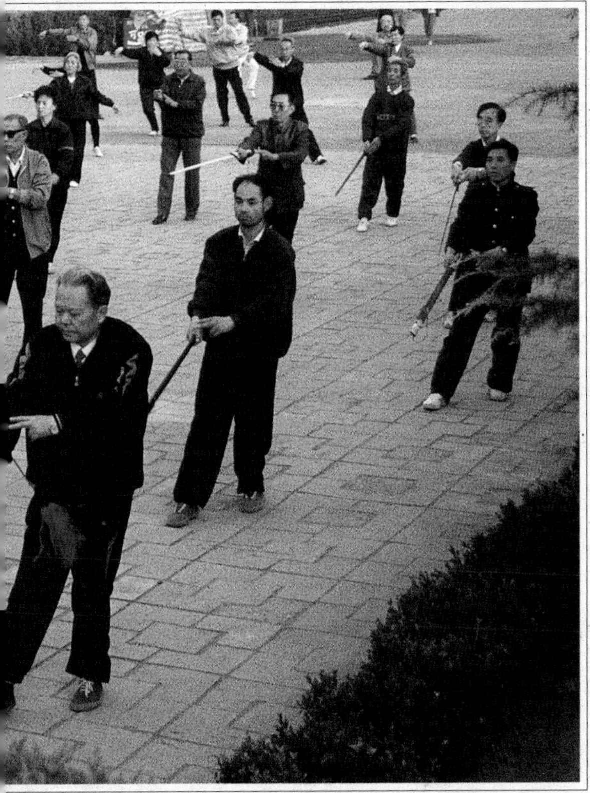

Internal martial arts involve soft, flowing, meditative movements that require no muscle tension.

to make use of relaxation and breathing techniques as a means of enhancing health and vitality.

The subsequent chapters each explore one of six main styles of internal martial arts, explaining its history, philosophy, and practice. The style that most people are familiar with is Taijiquan (also known as Tai Chi Chuan) which literally means "Yin Yang Fist." Less well known in the West, but very popular on mainland China, is the art of Baguazhang (also known as Pa Kwa Chang) meaning "Eight Triagram Palm." Also very common in the East, but rare in the West, is the Art of Xingyiquan (also known as Hsing I Chuan), which translates as "Form Intention Fist." The philosophies of these three main internal styles of ancient China are all intertwined with Daoism (see page 14).

The more modern soft style from Japan, Aikido, meaning "The Way of Spiritual Harmony" was created by Morihei Uyeshiba (1883-1969), who is acknowledged to be one of the greatest modern martial arts masters.

Finally, in Chapters 7 and 8, two less well-known but very important and influential internal styles from China are discussed. The first is the very rare Nine Little Heavens system, used by the students of its creator Wu Dao zi to guard the Daoist temples in the Tang Dynasty (A.D. 618-906). The second is the most concealed and hidden of all the internal martial arts, and possibly the one from which the rest derive: the 800-year-old Qi Disruption System of the Wudang Shan. It is still taught today by the 90-year-old leader of the Wudang Shan group, Liang Shih Kan, to a small band of students somewhere in the Wudang Shan mountain range.

The development of Qi energy flow around the body through the soft internal martial arts leads to a strong spirit and great longevity.

The Principles of the Internal Martial Arts

INTERNAL (SOFT) MARTIAL ARTS and external (hard) martial arts differ in many ways, but they also have much in common. This book is primarily concerned with internal martial arts, but here the benefits and limitations of both styles will be looked at in order to give a clear overview. I would strongly suggest that the principles presented in this book will benefit your training, whatever style you practice.

Most people involved in the martial arts usually share a common goal: to develop better self-defense skills; to improve general health; to develop oneself mentally, emotionally, and spiritually. The principles contained in this book aim to achieve all of these.

In recent years a gulf seems to have grown between the hard and soft styles, and in the West the two styles are often perceived as being on different sides of an impassable canyon. It is well known that today we associate the Buddhist Shaolin monastery exclusively with the hard styles, and the Daoists on Wudang Mountain with the soft styles. However, in ancient times this distinction between the two styles was not so clear, and many people trained in both soft as well as hard styles, whether at Shaolin or on Wudang Mountain. In China they maintain that the hard and soft styles are two different paths to the same place.

Hard stylists build up their Qi externally in the muscles and eventually make their training more relaxed to build up Qi in their internal organs. The hard styles, such as Karate and Shaolin Kung Fu, use movements that are linear and require muscle tension. Great power is developed in the limbs, but health is not cultivated to the same degree as in the soft styles. The hard styles concentrate mainly on developing external strength, which the Chinese call Li. This can be likened to the strength that is developed from playing sports or doing push-ups, or sit-ups, or from doing weight-training or any kind of cardiovascular activity.

Today, the hard and soft styles of the martial arts seem to have diverged, with the hard styles concentrating on the development of external strength.

Soft stylists build up Qi in their internal organs, encouraging it to flow out along the acupuncture meridians to the muscles. As they become more advanced, they make their

Practice in the hard styles should be balanced by internal training so that good health and mental balance are maintained.

training tougher to build up their external power, but for the first few years they concentrate on relaxation so that there should be no restriction to the flow of Qi. The soft styles use movements that are circular and flowing and require virtually no muscle tension at all. As a result, the flow of Qi energy is less restricted, and overall health is improved. The soft styles concentrate mainly on developing internal strength, which the Chinese call Jin (see page 35). The source of this strength is in the tendons, sinews, and ligaments.

It soon becomes clear that training in a combination of the two styles is ultimately preferable. If we constantly focus on the fitness of our superficial muscle power, the internal organs will be drained of energy and our health will decline. Conversely, if we concentrate only on nourishing our internal organs and neglect muscle tone, then our fitness will suffer. To really get the best from the martial arts, both the hard and soft styles should be trained, and this will develop both internal and external strength.

In ancient China, choice of training was traditionally a reflection of age: in general young people wanted greater Li (external strength), so they trained mostly in the hard styles and only a little in the soft styles. At the age of about thirty, they would begin to train equally in the soft styles, benefiting from the development of both Li and Jin. At sixty they would gradually reduce their hard style training, so that the body was still toned but not stressed, while the increased soft style training would ensure they were healthy enough to enjoy the autumn of their years. A balanced life was achieved with all the benefits of both Li, from hard style training, and Jin, from soft style training; and looking over their life, they could see a clear line of positive development.

Martial arts training should be a life-long program, so that the body, mind, and spirit are developed to their maximum potential.

THE PHILOSOPHY OF THE INTERNAL MARTIAL ARTS

This book is about the internal martial arts, not just as a means of self-defense, but also as a way of increasing internal energy and of developing body, mind, and spirit. Through training in the internal martial arts, our characters gradually change, and we concentrate less on how to defeat others and more on how to improve ourselves. All the internal arts are ways of self-cultivation, a type of moving meditation that can help us to see beyond the everyday and into the true nature of ourselves and the world around us.

In order to understand the philosophical concepts that lie behind the internal martial arts, it is necessary to be a little familiar with Daoism. Indeed, it is from Daoist theories that many of the practical principles of the internal martial arts evolved and were developed.

Many of the soft styles were created by Daoists living in seclusion in the mountain ranges of China. The Wudang mountain range is arguably the most famous, and this area is said to be the cradle of development of the ancient art of Taijiquan. Other important places include Emei Mountain, the birthplace of one of the branches of the internal martial art of Baguazhang.

The philosophy of Daoism, which is a part of everyone's life in China, emphasizes living in tune with nature.

THE INFLUENCE OF DAOISM

Daoism has been in existence in China for thousands of years. Its roots lie in prehistory, and, apart from a brief moment of recognition and prominence as the state religion under the reign of Emperor Tang Wu tsung in the seventh century, it has always been just one part of China's diverse religious beliefs, which are a mixture of Daoism, Buddhism, Confucianism, and Ancestor Worship.

Daoism has made a major contribution to China's cultural heritage. Daoist medical books form the basis of Traditional Chinese Medicine, which includes acupuncture, Chinese Herbal Medicine, Qigong, and acupressure massage. Daoist works of philosophy and spirituality have influenced all aspects of Chinese religious life. All these different strands are integral parts of the internal martial arts.

It is important that the Daoists should not be thought of as just a passive, nonviolent, intellectual influence in Chinese history. They were at one time a powerful political and effective military force. Indeed, toward the end of the second century A.D., the Daoist Yellow Hat Rebel Army fielded a force of over 350,000 men in an attempt to try to bring down the Han Dynasty.

Chinese herbalists have inherited their rich tradition from Daoism, one of the ancient religions practiced in China for thousands of years.

The essence of Daoism is that life should be lived in accordance with the ebb and flow of nature, and that everything on earth should be in tune with the spiritual force of Qi that animates all our lives. Dao means "the way," as in "the way of nature." To follow the Dao means to be aware of and in harmony with nature, then one's own Dao (own way) through life will be balanced and fulfilling.

Daoism teaches us about the ways of nature and how to use this knowledge to our advantage. Sometimes we "go with the flow," like water flowing down river to the sea. At other times we are as ferocious as a tiger and as devastating as a cyclone. We need to cultivate these Yin (passive) and Yang (active) qualities in ourselves and know when it is appropriate to apply them. We need to feel the Qi of a situation and respond to it with just the right balance of Yin and Yang.

Daoist books

There are three Daoist books that have strongly influenced the development of the internal martial arts. The first is The Yi jing, known in the West as the *Book of Changes*. It was written in 2852 B.C. by Fu Xi, and was further classified and organized in 1122 B.C. by Wen Wang, the first ruler of the state of Zhou.

Weng Wang said that Fu Xi had been able to formulate The Yi jing because he had spent a lifetime observing the energetic interaction of the sun, moon, and stars, and all the various forms that nature took here on earth. He had studied the behavior of animals and people, the changing of the weather and the seasons. He had observed all phenomena and had discerned the patterns within them expressed these as variations in the relationship of the forces of Yin and Yang.

The balancing of Yin and Yang is one of the main ideas in the internal martial arts. In the context of health, a Yin condition means there is a deficiency of Qi and therefore needs to be replenished. A Yang condition means there is an excess of Qi, which needs to be reduced. Balancing Yin and Yang in the body provides the key to good health, and the movements of the internal martial arts are designed to encourage this process.

The second important book in Daoism is Huang Di Nei Jing, known in the West as *The Yellow Emperor's Classic on Internal Medicine*. The Yellow Emperor lived from 2697 to 2597 B.C. and his great age is attributed to his knowledge of how the body is animated by Qi. This book contains the philosophy, principles, theories, and practical techniques that are the foundation of Traditional Chinese Medicine, Qigong, and the internal martial arts. The book explains how Yin and Yang simultaneously support and oppose each other, how Ching (essence), Qi (energy), and Shen (spirit) transform into one another and about the interaction of the Five Elements of Wood, Fire, Earth, Metal, and Water . All these different Daoist philosophies feature very heavily in the principles and practice of the various styles and forms of internal martial arts.

Lao Zi, who wrote *The Way of Virtue*, encouraged practitioners to develop a virtuous character.

The third important Daoist book that has also had a strong influence on the internal martial arts is the Dao De Jing, known in the West as *The Way of Virtue*. It was written in the sixth century B.C. by Lao Zi, whose name literally means "wise old man." He clearly enjoyed his anonymity, and this is reflected in his book: he encourages the avoidance of arrogance and egotism, and stresses the cultivation of virtuous behavior and peacefulness. The book is a series of short verses that poetically express some of the ideas of Daoism, and that are clearly reflected in the internal martial arts. For instance, one verse describes how, if we allow ourselves to become stiff and tense, like old, dry wood that is brittle and inflexible, then we are courting death. However, if we are flexible and supple, like young bamboo, then we will have long, healthy lives.

Lao Zi stressed the importance of cultivating virtuous behavior. All those who practice the internal martial arts follow this code. We train to build ourselves up rather than bring others down, and we only use the fighting aspects of our art in order to defend ourselves when we are attacked. We aim not only to develop good self-defense skills, but also to cultivate a compassionate and virtuous character, to improve health physically, emotionally, and mentally, and to enhance and develop the spirit. At an advanced level, the internal martial arts are not something that we do, they are something that we live.

MOVING MEDITATION

In addition to developing Jin (internal strength),the forms of the soft martial arts are also a type of moving meditation. Meditation is a way of entering a state in which the conscious mind is not active while still remaining awake. The mind, which is usually constantly active while we are awake and also when we dream, benefits enormously from the chance to rest and will be revitalized when we do start to use it again. Just as an overworked body needs time to recuperate by relaxing with a vacation, so the mind needs rest in order to function properly. This is why meditation is so important. In order to maintain good health, we need to rest both the mind and body.

Meditation is vital to the internal martial arts, because, in the absence of conscious thought a space is created that can then be filled by our spirit.

During moving meditation the flow of Qi through the body should be smooth and continuous like water in a stream.

Our spirit brings us insights into our lives, so we can continue to grow and develop our understanding of ourselves and the world around us. Sometimes we might be given an insight into how to change or enhance our lives, or we might be given information or an awareness that will help us succeed in a chosen field.

When we give the spirit more space, we start to perceive the world in a different way. This is sometimes a literal change of perception, like developing the ability to see Qi energy. It can also be a change in perception that is not to do with sight, but with the process of perception itself. Such a transformation is very hard to define, because it is a state of being rather than a thought or a feeling. It can be likened to the moment when one suddenly realizes the answer to a problem, or when a lost memory is suddenly recovered. It is the moment of a flash of inspiration, a moment of realization or enlightenment.

These types of shifts in perception are attainable through meditation. The word meditation usually conjures up a picture of a person sitting cross-legged and motionless on the floor. However, the internal martial arts use moving meditation, which has many benefits for the body, mind, and spirit that are not possible with sitting meditation.

When we are moving through the forms of the internal martial arts, the subconscious mind is totally focused on controlling and coordinating the body in order to perform the movements of the various self-defense applications. It cannot intrude on the space we have created for our spirit. Some people find that during a sitting meditation, the subconscious mind fills the space created by the absence of the conscious mind with old memories and habitual thought patterns, leaving our spirit no room to manifest itself.

The great benefit of a moving meditation is that we can bring it into our everyday lives and it can be something that we associate with normal activity, rather than something completely separate from our lives.

We should not have to try and meditate while doing the forms of the internal martial arts. If we are training correctly, then the Qi flow we generate will carry us effortlessly into the meditative state, just like a stream flowing into the ocean. Indeed, this simile is an appropriate way of describing moving meditation, because the movements should be soft and continuously moving.

The soft style practitioner is drawn effortlessly into moving meditation, where the spirit is freed and insights are gained.

This is in contrast to the hard styles where one move follows another rather than in a continuous flow of movement. These external, stiff movements influence the mind, which also becomes fixed rather than flowing. In fact, many practitioners of the hard styles are encouraged to commit totally to a technique with all of the conscious mind and to be completely focused on the punch or kick that they are training.

Peripheral Vision

The internal martial arts do not use the conscious mind for fighting. All responses are a subconscious reflex instead.

This is best illustrated by explaining the different way in which the eyes are used. Whereas the external martial arts stress the use of Focus Vision, or looking at the opponent, the internal martial arts emphasize the use of Periphery Vision, or awareness of the space displaced by the presence of the opponent. Focus Vision is directly linked to the conscious mind, and hard stylists always depend on conscious thought. This has two drawbacks: first, it may mean when one is fighting, vital time is wasted thinking of what technique to use next and consequently the response to the attack may be too slow; second, if the conscious mind is active during training, there is no room for the spirit to manifest itself.

Peripheral Vision, however, connects with the subconscious mind. When we are attacked, we react immediately: no conscious thought is involved, and there is no time delay and our chance of success is increased. Furthermore, during training there will be no thoughts to crowd us, only an empty space that can be filled by our spirit.

SPIRITUAL DEVELOPMENT

According to ancient Daoist theory, we have three treasures within us: Ching (essence), Qi (lifeforce energy), and Shen (spirit). In the internal martial arts we can transform Ching, into Qi, and then into Shen.

Ching has many different meanings. It describes the nutrient substances in the body that are derived from food. It is also a component of our inherited genetic potential, as well as an aspect of our sexual creative force connected to our hormones.

Qi (lifeforce energy) has many different meanings, too (see also page 28). It is the electromagnetic and electro-chemical energy that flows around the body through the acupuncture meridians. It is also the functional power of the internal organs.

To transform Ching to Qi, heat is required, and this is generated during training or the deep abdominal breathing (see page 24) of the internal martial arts. The heat generated is like a fire, which heats the water (Ching) that produces the steam (Qi). One could say that if the body was a steam engine, then Ching (essence) is like the water and Qi (lifeforce energy) is the steam that powers the machine, the body.

Developing the spirit (Shen) fires the imagination and stimulates creativity – it is an exciting and uplifting process.

The transformational process of Ching to Qi to Shen means that, as well as our spirits being a force that existed prior to our physical birth, they are also the result of an ongoing process of development as we grow and experience life.

The transformational process of Ching to Qi to Shen can be represented symbolically if we imagine that there is a cauldron in the belly that contains our Ching. When this is heated, through exercise and deep abdominal breathing (see page 24), steam rises from the cauldron and expands throughout the whole body in the form of Qi. On reaching the head, this warm mist condenses and rains back down into the cauldron in the belly to be reheated. Once this process has been happening for a while, a very fine vaporlike energy collects in the head: this is Shen.

Another way to describe the process is to imagine that the body is a candle. The melted wax at the base of the wick is Ching, the heat of the flame is Qi, and the light is Shen. As we go through life, our light shines and we make the world a brighter place. In the fast pace of Western society, there is a tendency for people to "burn twice as bright for half as long" or to "burn the candle at both ends." However, the Daoist approach has always been one of moderation and of avoiding extremes so that a long life can be enjoyed in good health, with time to cultivate and develop the spirit.

Shen means several different things. In one sense it is a mental and creative power. Indeed, people who train the internal martial arts find that they have more mental power available to achieve their aims, whether they are business or leisure. They find that they are more inspired to develop creative projects, such as painting, music, or writing.

Shen also has a more literal meaning: it refers to the "spirit body." This is a duplicate of the physical body, but instead of having veins with blood flowing through them, it has acupuncture meridians with Qi flowing through them. The idea of the physical body containing a duplicate spirit body is a concept which is difficult for some people to grasp, but it can be likened to the different states of water, ice, and steam.

Ice is a solid substance, but it can transform into water and become a flowing liquid. It can transform further into steam and, as a gas, can rise up into the sky. Ice, water, and steam are all the same thing in a different state. A person is much the same in relation to their spirit. After many years of practice, the physical body becomes less stiff and starts to flow through the forms of the internal martial arts – like ice to water, Ching to Qi. As the movements start to feel effortless, a sensation of weightlessness and expansion beyond the self is experienced – this is like water becoming steam, Qi becoming Shen.

We should endeavor to develop ourselves until we feel as familiar with our spirit body as we do with our physical body, and we should aim to achieve a state where we are able to fly in our spirit body as naturally as we walk in our physical body.

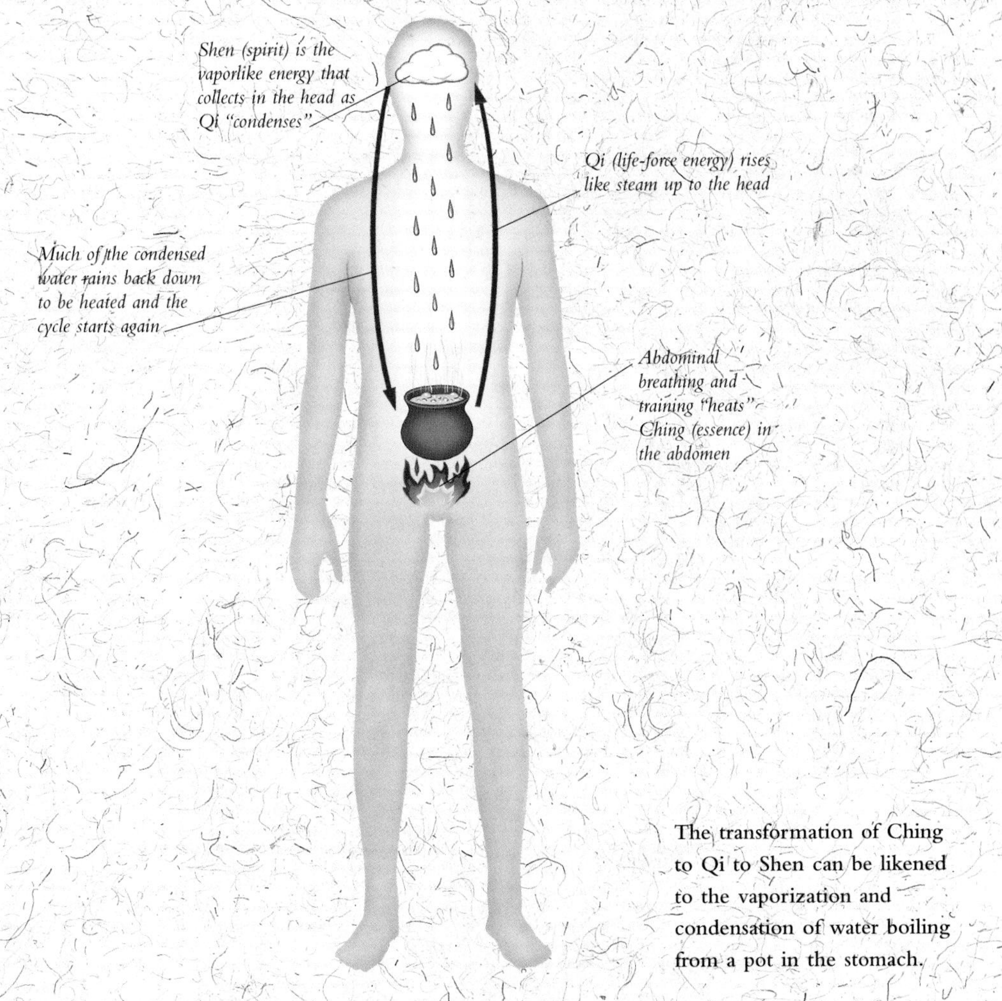

Shen (spirit) is the vaporlike energy that collects in the head as Qi "condenses"
Qi (life-force energy) rises like steam up to the head
Much of the condensed water rains back down to be heated and the cycle starts again
Abdominal breathing and training "heats" Ching (essence) in the abdomen

The transformation of Ching to Qi to Shen can be likened to the vaporization and condensation of water boiling from a pot in the stomach.

STRENGTHENING THE WILL

Strength of will is an aspect of the spirit rather than the mind. In extreme situations it makes the difference between life and death. There is a well-known story that illustrates this, where, after a serious road accident, a child ends up trapped under the wheel of a truck. With no one around to help, the child's mother manages to lift the truck enough to free her daughter and save her life.

This story illustrates how, in unusual circumstances, we can summon up great strength that would normally be inaccessible. It was the mother's strength of will that saved her daughter's life. It is possible through advanced training in the self-defense aspects of the internal martial arts to actually cultivate this ability.

During self-defense training there is a slow buildup of pressure from our opponent, which we have to counter, not just physically, with blocks and counterstrikes, but also by our strength of will. As the pressure increases and the opponent's blows come harder and faster, it is only by summoning up our deepest untapped potential that we can succeed and not succumb.

In the internal martial arts there are many two-person prearranged fighting sequences that cultivate strength of will and develop the spring-like power of Jin (internal force). The pressure applied by the opponent to us is like a spring being compressed and given potential energy that it can then release. If we have to block a punch, we must generate at least as much power in our block as the opponent has in their punch; otherwise, he or she will get through our defense and hit us. After many years of training, the repeated effect of generating a force to match the opponent's, like two springs pressing against each other, strengthens our bodies and our Jin, as well as our strength of will. Another important benefit of training in the internal martial arts as a self-defense system is that not only can we defend ourselves and our families and friends in times of danger, but in peaceful times we can enjoy the sense of self-confidence and achievement that comes from the strengthening of the will. It enables us to think clearly and make sensible, rational decisions, even when we are under pressure, rather than letting our lives be ruled by emotional turmoil and confusion.

Clear thinking can be likened to clear water. Extreme emotions stir up the water and muddy it so that things become obscured. We should listen to our emotions and make use of the power they give us. However, we should also use our strength of will to make sure we are not ruled by them and that our thoughts remain clear.

We can use an example from our internal martial arts training to see how the principle can be applied in daily life. Imagine an opponent is about to attack. At such a moment we experience a combination of fear and anger, both of which release vast amounts of energy into our system. If we know how, we can use our strength of will to channel this emotionally generated energy in to a counterstrike to help us defeat the opponent. However, if we are not familiar with this experience, then the emotions can be overwhelming and could result in our being frozen on the spot or succumbing to irrational behavior.

To apply this principle to everyday life, we should imagine a time at work or at home when someone says something that "presses our buttons," i.e., stirs us up emotionally. Instead of letting ourselves be overcome by our emotions and making an irrational and nonbeneficial comment, we can apply what we have learned from our internal martial arts training, and use our strength of will while under this psychological pressure to maintain clear thinking, so our verbal response is one that resolves the situation to our advantage.

Two-person training exercises give us a greater understanding of timing, distance, and sensitivity to other people's energy, which is beneficial not just for self-defense, but also for developing the ability to relate to other people in everyday life, to be more aware of when their Qi is "up" and they are happy, buoyant, and joyful, or when their Qi is "down" and they are sad, depressed, or melancholy.

When practicing the solo forms of the internal martial arts, if we imagine the self-defense applications of the moves, the body then thinks it has more work to do, and releases and circulates more energy, so the health benefit is greater. Also, when we train, if our attitude is to defeat the opponent, the body will apply this intention internally as well, and will defeat harmful viruses and bacteria. Furthermore, when we train to strengthen the will, the body's resistance to illness is increased. Tests have shown that a positive attitude not only defeats nonbeneficial thought patterns, but also boosts the immune system.

In the modern world of high pressure and fast living, stress and its resultant diseases are a greater threat to our life than muggers and thieves. If we can maintain good health, then we can achieve final victory over our opponents by outliving them!

Developing strength of will through practicing the soft martial arts will enable us to channel our energy to overcome stressful situations in our everday lives

RELAXATION

There is a great deal of pressure, both physical and psychological, involved in all the self-defense aspects of the internal martial arts, but at no time should we allow our muscles or minds to be tense. The ability to remain relaxed under pressure, but still achieve our objectives, is also of great benefit in everyday life. It becomes a subconscious response we can use for any situation that we encounter in life, not only physical but also verbal, mental, or emotional. Indeed, internal martial arts can be practiced not only as a form of stress release, but also as a system of avoiding stress in the first place. All these things are possible because when we train we are relaxed.

Through internal martial arts training, not only can stress be reduced, but it can be avoided completely.

In the two-person fighting forms, the opponent is encouraged to gradually increase the force, the speed, and the power of their attacks, while we continue to counterattack, remaining relaxed throughout. In this way we develop the ability to stay calm and relaxed even when we are under great physical and psycho-logical stress and pressure.

From a self-defense point of view, by avoiding excessive tension in the limbs, it is possible to extend them smoothly in a strike. Muscle contraction restricts punches and strikes, and gives away our intentions to our opponent.

This difference between the internal and the external styles also influences our health. The external martial arts build up Qi in the arms and legs through the intentional contraction of these muscles. In the internal martial arts Qi is generated in the torso by special abdominal breathing (see page 24). It is then channeled into the arms and legs using vigorous waist rotations which, in turn, generate a centrifugal force that carries the Qi out to the extremities (hands and feet). The flow of Qi is not restricted by

The unimpeded circulation of Qi around the body and to all its extremities is central to the soft martial arts.

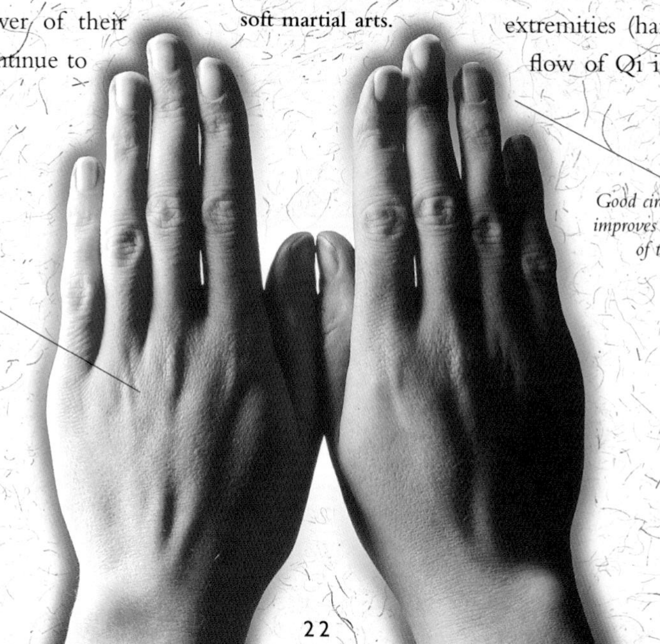

Good circulation of Qi results in good health

Good circulation of Qi improves the circulation of the blood

Cardiovascular training is good for general fitness but neglects internal health and may result in energy loss.

any unnecessary muscle tension, and this combination of centrifugal waist power and relaxation improves the circulation of the blood.

Furthermore, the release of physical tension allows the release of mental tension, so we are able to really relax on all levels. Stress is a contributing factor in many serious illnesses, such as stomach ulcers, insomnia, and migraine, as well as lifethreatening medical conditions like heart attacks. Many people suffering from general aches and pains due to the stresses and strains of everyday life experience great improvements to their general health once they begin daily training in the internal martial arts. They develop an internal strength that helps them cope with the pressures of life, so they do not get so run down.

Many people mistakenly do external martial arts, weight training, or cardiovascular training as a way of countering stress and staying healthy. However, while these activities improve general fitness, they do not benefit health. They build up external strength, but can leave you feeling hollow and weak on the inside. Such training not only drains the internal organs in order to supply the body's external musculature with energy, but it also means a constant expenditure of energy.

External training should always be balanced by internal martial arts, where Qi is accumulated rather than spent and the sensation of feeling substantial and strong inside can be enjoyed. In a relaxed body Qi can circulate freely both internally and externally. As a result, not only are the muscles nourished and strengthened, but so are the important internal organs, and it is these that ultimately determine strength and health.

Good health can be maintained by daily training in the movements of the internal martial arts, and these encourage the flow of Qi through the acupuncture meridians of the body (see page 29) clearing away any blockages caused by tension. This process can actually be felt in the body: areas of blocked Qi feel stiff and achy, while flowing, healing Qi feels like a pleasant, warm electric glow spreading through the body. As the healing Qi moves, it pushes ahead of it the stagnant energy until it is cleared from the body entirely, it is then that one feels refreshed with a sense of calmness and well-being. The whole body feels warm, full, and at peace.

BREATHING

Another way in which we can increase Qi flow to improve health is through the use of special breathing techniques. These are fundamental to the internal martial arts, and breathing can be used to regulate the body, mind, emotions, energy, and spirit that are all interconnected. A common example of how people use the breath to help them regulate their restless minds and untamed emotions happens when they have become panicked and their breath has become short and rapid. They take long, slow, deep breaths and exhale through the mouth to calm down.

The breathing techniques of the internal martial arts are centered around the abdomen area rather than the chest. The chest is usually kept relaxed, and the abdomen is expanded and contracted by the inhalation and exhalation of the breath. The Lower Dan Dien energy center (see page 34), situated just below and behind the navel, is activated by this type of breathing, and Qi can go from there to all other parts of the body.

There are four general benefits that can be gained from using abdominal breathing techniques. First, it generates more Qi in the whole body, just like pumping up a balloon. Second, the whole abdominal area becomes stronger and more able to resist blows. Third, the internal organs are massaged by this movement, which will make them stronger and better able to function. Finally, abdominal breathing helps to pump the Qi around the body along the circuit known as The Small Circulation of Qi (see page 29).

Inhale, allowing the breath to expand the abdomen naturally

The Buddhist breathing technique is not only essential in self-defense applications, but is also energizing, promoting good health and vitality.

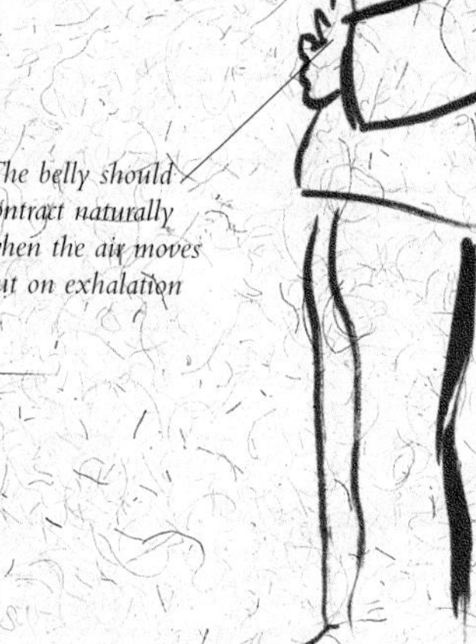

The belly should contract naturally when the air moves out on exhalation

There are two major types of abdominal breathing used in internal martial arts: Buddhist breathing, where the belly expands on inhalation and contracts on exhalation, and the more advanced technique known as Daoist breathing, where the abdomen is contracted on inhalation and expanded on exhalation.

Abdominal breathing should be practiced and mastered before it is introduced into the forms. The following practice can be done either sitting or standing. Beginning with the Buddhist breathing technique, put the palms of your hands on your navel and then, as you inhale, allow the feeling of your breath to expand the abdomen. Feel it pressing against the palms of your hands, but don't push your belly out. Allow it to happen naturally. As you exhale, feel your belly contract. Again, don't pull in – just allow it to move naturally. When you have mastered this, put it into your internal martial arts forms. After a few years you will be ready to start practicing the Daoist breathing technique.

The abdominal movement for both techniques is a result of the breath moving the belly, not muscle tension and contraction. With both types of breathing, the inhalation, exhalation, and accompanying abdominal movement is done in coordination with the extension and retraction of the arms and legs. When the hands and feet move away from the body for a punch or a kick, there should always be an exhalation. This gives more power to counterattacks and helps Qi to flow from the Lower Dan Dien out along the acupuncture meridians, to the tips of the fingers, toes, and head, and then back to the Lower Dan Dien.

The belly is contracted on inhalation, but do not use force

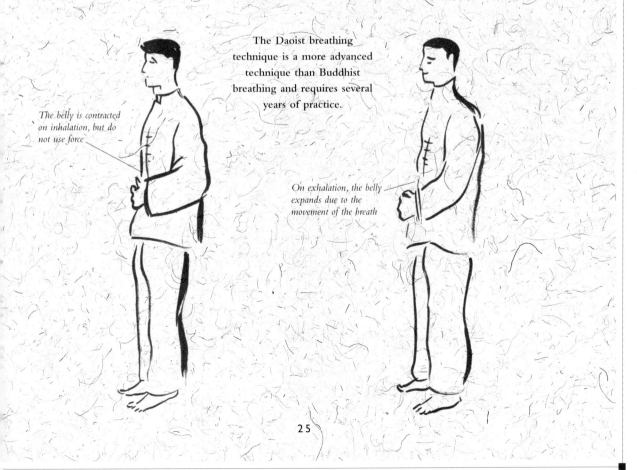

The Daoist breathing technique is a more advanced technique than Buddhist breathing and requires several years of practice.

On exhalation, the belly expands due to the movement of the breath

ROOTING

Another source of power in internal martial arts training is called Rooting. This is what gives us our strong connection with the ground, like the roots of a tree. Rooting is not just good for greater physical stability when using the martial arts applications; it also improves mental and emotional stability and creates an energetic and spiritual connection with the earth.

To develop Rooting, you have to physically sink your body weight down into the lower body by bending the knees and imagining that your main body weight is in your lower belly and legs, not in your chest and head. Relax and try to lower your center of gravity in order to achieve greater stability. When the knees are bent, the legs have to support our body weight. This helps the development of Jin (internal strength) in the legs. With the knees slightly bent the Lower Dan Dien (see page 34) is also activated.

The feet should grip the ground like claws while the legs push against the ground. As we shift our body weight from leg to leg, one expands, and the other compresses, releasing their coiled energy like springs.

One of the most common stances in internal martial arts is the Bow and Arrow stance. This stance derives its name from the appearance of the legs when the weight is forward. The front leg is bent like a bow, while the back leg is straight like an arrow. Just as a bow releases its

Like the roots of a tree connected deep into the earth, practicing rooting will connect us with the earth's energy.

power into an arrow, a dynamic, explosive strength is released from the internal power of the legs into the arms. The muscles are relaxed, but the tendons are always slightly flexed, like a bow string on a long bow which has a flex in it, even when it is not being drawn to fire an arrow.

In addition to rooting us to the ground, our feet provide a vital interchange point for Qi passing from the earth to the body.

When properly rooted it is possible to move others but remain unmoved. Rooting is also the key to balance when using grappling, locking, controlling, and throwing techniques. For Fa jin strikes (see page 36) we can get great power from the waist; however, if we add the Rooting principles, we will have even more power. To try to release Fa jin without Rooting is like trying to push a car wearing roller-skates.

It is highly beneficial to practice internal martial arts barefoot on grass in order to draw Qi energy up from the earth into the body through the soles of the feet. This exchange is done through the acupuncture point Kidney One, which is located on the sole of the foot and is also known in Chinese as the Bubbling Spring.

It is also possible to send energy into the ground, like the roots of a tree, and exchange energy with the earth. This has a great healing benefit both physically and spiritually. Also, as the energy in the body increases and our connection with the earth deepens, we start to see nature in a new way. The colors of the plants, flowers, and trees become brighter and deeper. The songs of birds and calls of other creatures become clearer. Most wonderful of all, as our energy expands and blends with the energy of the natural world, a communication is established and an interaction and connection is formed with the greater Spirit of Nature of which we are a part. Qi connects the mind and body together with each other and the world. Qi is what the strands of the web of life are made of.

Mental and emotional stability comes from a sense of "at oneness" with the forces of nature.

QI: ENERGY OF THE INTERNAL MARTIAL ARTS

To discuss the internal martial arts without discussing Qi would be like trying explain radios, televisions, and computers without mentioning electricity. Qi is easiest to comprehend if it is thought of as a type of electromagnetic or electrochemical force. It feels like glowing, warm, electric water flowing through the body. The internal martial arts heal the body by encouraging the production of more Qi and by increasing its flow around the body through the acupuncture meridians (see opposite). The electric charges that are involved are very small, just as when two people touch and there is a small static electricity spark.

In the same way that electricity allows a radio to produce sound, a television to produce images, and a bulb to produce light, Qi enables us to move, see, and speak. All the different things that people can do is because of their Qi. The more Qi we have, the more active we can be and the more we can achieve.

It was the early Daoists who, over four thousand years ago, through their observations of nature became aware of Qi. They developed movement and breathing exercises based on the natural movements of animals and the principles of Yin and Yang to increase and balance their own Qi.

Qi can heal not only the body, but also the emotions. Often a person with a tendency toward anxiety, or who is feeling down and lacking self-confidence, is simply experiencing an insufficiency of Qi. When a person cultivates their Qi, they start to feel more substantial, confident, and strong.

The exercises that are designed to cultivate Qi are called Qigong. Today there are over two thousand different types of Qigong. The Daoists used Qigong exercises as a way of improving their health and increasing longevity. They helped them balance their Yin and Yang energies and develop their spirits. The internal martial arts developed as a result of Qigong movement and breathing principles being incorporated into already existing martial arts systems. Some Qigong systems have even been adapted to become internal martial arts.

Qigong postures balance and regulate the energy in the meridians (right) and bring the energy into the Dan Dien (left) where it is stored.

ACUPUNCTURE MERIDIANS

When we are young, all our acupuncture meridians are open and the flow of Qi through them is very strong. We seem to have unlimited energy and can laugh, cry, and run around for hours and hours. As we get older, we acquire mental and physical tension that causes the flow of Qi through the channels to be greatly reduced. Qi flow is reduced by poor diet, bad lifestyle, illness, and extreme mental and emotional states.

By training in the internal martial arts, we can increase the flow of Qi through the acupuncture meridians, which strengthens the body's resistance to illness and improves general health and well-being. With regularly training it is possible to regain the vitality and dynamism of youth.

The acupuncture meridians run throughout the entire body, connecting every part of it. There are twelve major meridians named after the internal organs to which they are connected. The internal organs can be thought of as reservoirs of energy, and the meridians as rivers that flow from them. The twelve meridians pass through the internal organs and extend to the tips of the toes, the top of the head, and the ends of the fingers. There are eight more meridians that connect the twelve main organ meridians together and regulate the amount of Qi in them. In addition, the eight extra meridians can also be used to store excess energy that is generated through training in the internal martial arts.

Two of the eight extra meridians are of particular importance to internal martial arts practitioners. These are the Conception meridian, which is situated on the midline of the front of the body, and the Governing Meridian situated on the midline of the back of the body. If we touch the tongue to the roof of our mouth, these two meridians are connected to each other and the Qi can flow in a circuit around the body to be more evenly distributed. This circuit is commonly known as The Small Circulation of Qi.

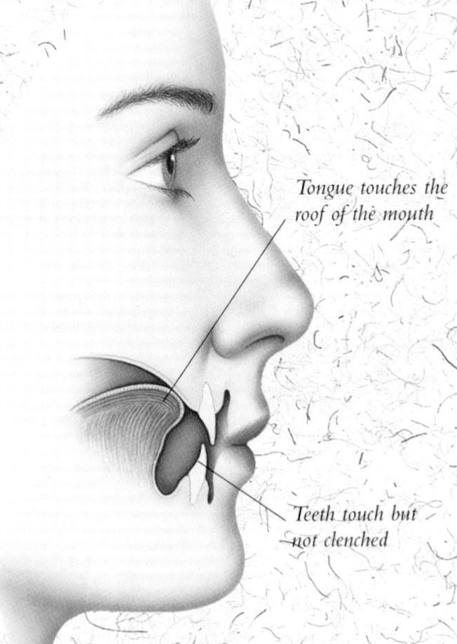

The Governing Meridian and Conception Meridian are connected when the tongue touches the roof of the mouth.

Acupuncture meridians are not nerves or blood vessels, nor are they part the lymphatic system. However, they can influence these and all other body organs and systems because they run through them all. If the body was cut open, the acupuncture meridians could not be seen because they are not like physical electric cables. The acupuncture meridians are in fact the pathways of least electrical resistance in the body.

There are a number of processes by which energy travels through the body along the meridians. When it travels through the nervous system, it is through the activity of the neurones.

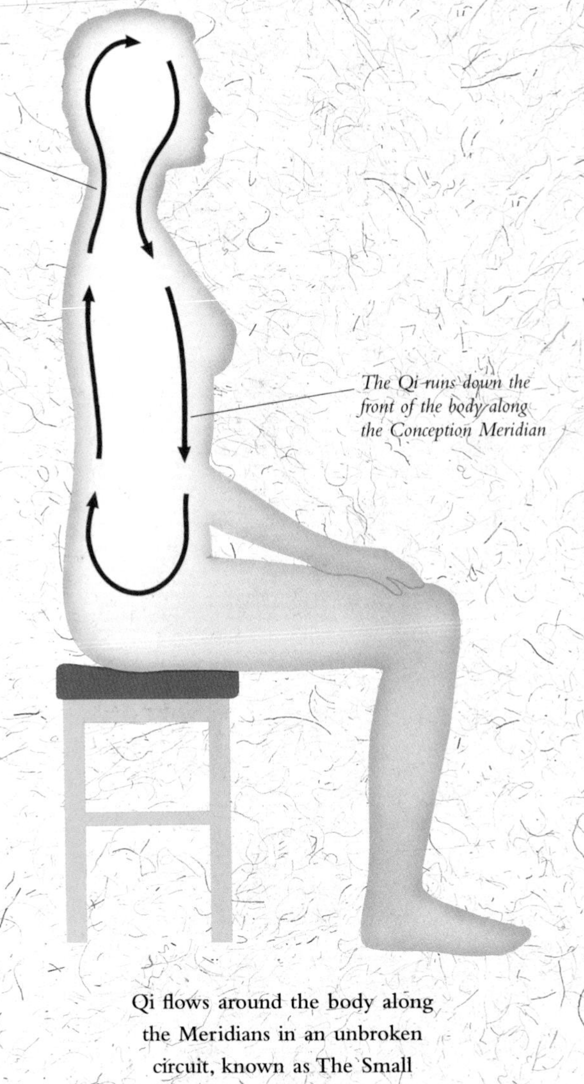
The Governing Meridian runs up the back of the body
The Qi runs down the front of the body along the Conception Meridian

Qi flows around the body along the Meridians in an unbroken circuit, known as The Small Circulation of Qi.

When it travels through the body fluids, it is through the ionic transfer of electrons. When energy travels through the tissue, it is via the cell membrane, which has selective protein pumps that can pump positive ions to one side and negative ions to the other side. This creates a potential difference across the membrane, thus producing a current.

The existence of the acupuncture meridian system is not in doubt. The World Health Organization of the United Nations went so far as publishing a report ("A proposed standard international acupuncture nomenculture," WHO 1991) detailing over 400 acupuncture points and the 20 meridians. They recognize this as a healthcare system and are keen to see its use become more widespread.

ACUPUNCTURE POINTS

Acupuncture points are the high-electric conductance points on the body where the flow of Qi can be most easily influenced. When electrical skin resistance is measured, we find that all these points have a lower resistance than the surrounding skin. Some acupuncturists exploit this effect by using electronic "point finders" in order to locate acupoints to the millimeter.

In 1991 a Superconducting Quantum Interference Device was used to map the lines of the force-fields of electromagnetic energy generated by the human body. They were found to correspond exactly with the acupuncture meridians and acupuncture points that were documented by the Chinese more than two and a half thousand years ago.

Acupuncture points can be needled by an acupuncturist to heal a wide variety of ailments. In ancient China practitioners of the internal martial arts traditionally practiced acupuncture and herbalism as well. They practiced internal martial arts to keep their own Qi flowing so they would be healthy and strong enough to heal others, and they taught their arts to their students so the knowledge would not be lost.

Today much of the knowledge held by the ancient practicioners is fragmented. Fortunately, however, with the development of better world-wide communications, the apparently diverse strands of Chinese acupuncture, Chinese Herbal Medicine, Qigong, and internal martial arts are coming together again to form the single unified subject that they once were in ancient times.

Qi can be emitted through the palm in both healing and self-defense strikes.

Acupuncture point Pericardium Eight

Many of the movements and postures of the internal martial arts forms often seem odd in appearance and have no clear meaning or application. This is because they are not simple blocks and strikes like in other martial arts. The strange movements are to position oneself in order to be able to access certain acupuncture points on the opponent's body. This is the highest level of self-defense. Strikes to the opponent's acupuncture points are done with a type of explosive technique called Fa jin (see page 36).

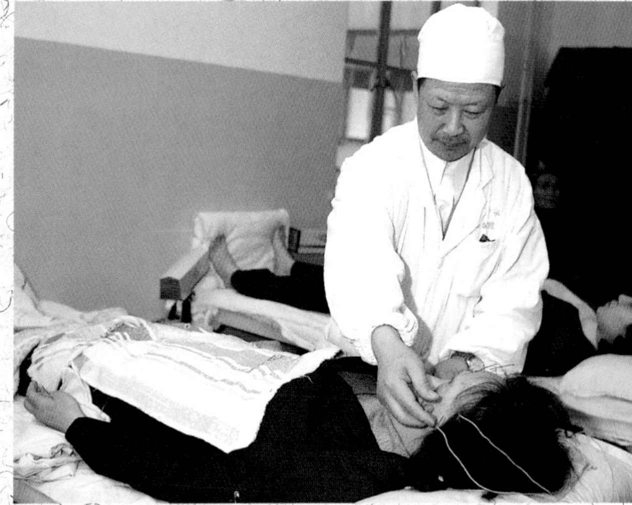

Unblocking the Qi is part of both the acupuncturist's art and that of the internal martial arts practitioner.

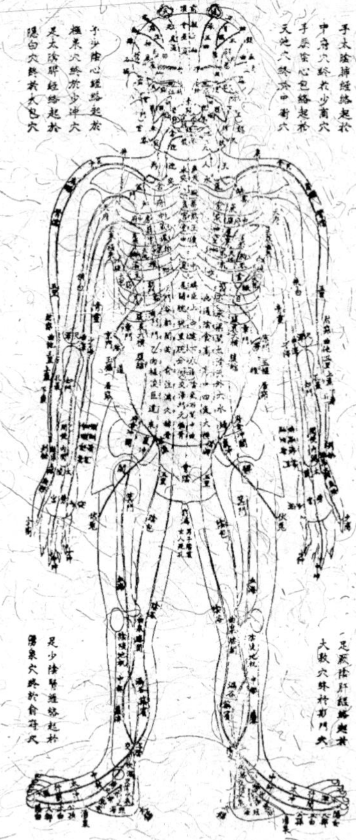

Modern scientific methods can now identify the acupuncture points of the body, but Chinese practitioners have produced identical maps for thousands of years.

A practitioner of the internal martial arts can release his or her Qi energy into the strikes to give them more power. Qi is most often released through a point called Pericardium Eight on the palm of the hand.

The ability to emit Qi is not only used to fight people, it is also used as healing force, with practitioners emitting healing Qi energy from their hands to heal their students, as well as anyone who has an ailment or needs an energy boost.

Recent tests at the Shanghai Atomic Nuclear Institute in China confirmed the ability of certain internal martial arts Masters to be able to emit Qi energy. They registered low-frequency fluctuating carrier waves that were emitted from the palms of practitioners of the internal martial arts. This Qi energy was detected as a microparticle flow which measured 60 microns in diameter, and had a velocity of 8–18 inches per second. ("The human energy field in relation to science, consciousness and health", http://www.vxm.com, 1996)

Through internal martial arts training, a powerful healing art is learned. Ultimately the goal is not just to be able to heal the patient, but to teach them the internal martial arts so that they can, in turn, increase and maintain their own heath. Different postures from the internal martial arts are well known to have the ability to heal particular ailments and illnesses, and it is not unusual for students or patients to be prescribed a series of movements as a course of treatment to be practiced several times a day.

QI EXPERIENCES

It is important for new students to the internal martial arts to know what Qi is and how they are likely to experience it.

When Qi flows around the body, it feels like a warm, electric glow. In the areas where Qi flow is blocked or stagnated, there will be an ache or a pain. These areas may be the location of an old injury, or they may be the areas where physical tension has built up due to daily mental tension. They identify the location of a health problem. Whatever the cause, these areas will eventually clear as Qi flow increases, until the whole body feels warm, healed, and strong. Some people who have accumulated unexpressed emotions may find they are pushed to the surface during training by the increased Qi flow. At such times it is best just to let them out rather than suppressing them deeper. If shouting or crying occur, it is anger and sadness being released. Other emotions are released in different ways. When the emotions are cleared, it is not unusual to find oneself gently laughing. (This is very nice, although if you are practicing in a public place passersby may think you are a bit odd!) Emotions, if not released, will block Qi flow, and this could lead to an illness developing later. It is well known that emotional and physiological pressure (stress) can cause serious ailments such as heart attacks and stomach ulcers.

People say that they feel Qi as a warm, electrical tingling sensation in their fingertips and other parts of the body. When a meridian is activated, it is possible to feel its line of force through the body. After practicing for a certain amount of time, it feels as if an electromagnetic force field is building up around the hands and body.

These very pleasant and enjoyable sensations are often accompanied by a sense of weightlessness, as if in zero gravity or swimming through the air. At its highest level the experience is as if one were made of warm, electric, liquid mercury.

At the end of a training session, not only has the flow of Qi helped heal the body, but it has also helped to balance the mind and emotions, and strengthen the spirit.

Practicing the internal martial arts is a good preparation for the day ahead, restoring Qi flow and releasing emotions.

STORING QI

After a training session it is very important to store the Qi we have generated in the energy center called the Lower Dan Dien, located just below and behind the navel. This is a bit like recharging the body's main battery.

Place the palms on the lower belly just below the navel and then, concentrating on the lower belly, imagine the Qi energy spiraling into this area. After a minute or two, a warm fullness sensation in the lower belly is experienced. This means that the Qi has been stored in the Lower Dan Dien.

As time goes by, more and more energy is stored and accumulated. This helps strengthen the body's resistance and provides a reserve that can be called upon in times of need.

To understand the importance of gathering and accumulating Qi, think of a car tire, which can support the great weight of the car overhead because of the strong internal air pressure inside it pushing out.

Day-to-day pressures and stress from our personal lives and at work all take their toll, and colds, flu, and other illnesses constantly stress the system. The best way to counter this variety of weights that knock us down daily is to have a greater internal pressure pushing out.

Just like air pressure in the car tire, Qi pressure in the body keeps one buoyant and prevents one from going under. It also radiates outward, preventing illness and stress getting in, as well as brightening up the lives of the people with whom we share our lives.

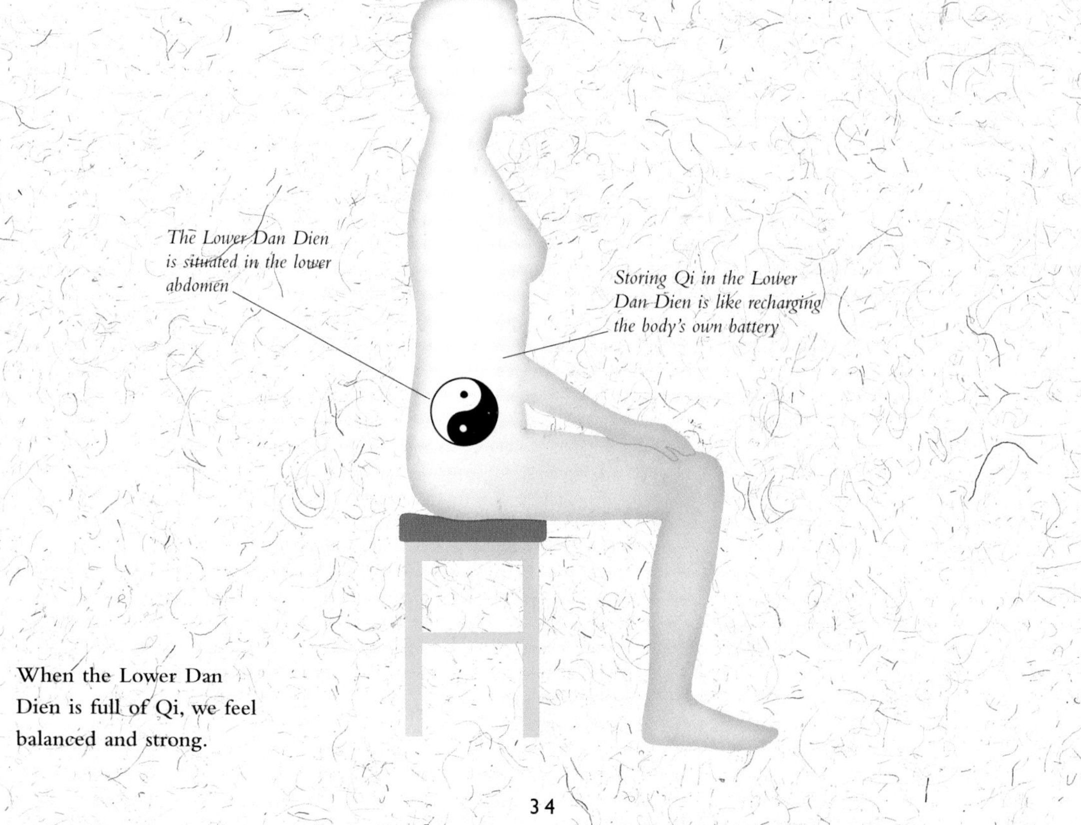
The Lower Dan Dien is situated in the lower abdomen
Storing Qi in the Lower Dan Dien is like recharging the body's own battery

When the Lower Dan Dien is full of Qi, we feel balanced and strong.

JIN: INTERNAL FORCE

In addition to developing Qi, the internal martial arts also develop Jin, which means "internal strength" or "internal force." This is a type of heavy, loose, relaxed, elastic, whole-body power, originating not so much from the muscles, but from a combination of the tendons, ligaments and sinews, and acupuncture meridians.

To best understand Jin, think about the difference between an axeman chopping down a tree and a carpenter hammering in a single nail. The axeman uses his whole body in an integrated way, making use of his waist rotation and leg power, as well as his arms, in each of his cutting strokes. The carpenter, on the other hand, uses only his arm each time he strikes.

The advantage of having Jin as part of one's self-defense system is that it gives the techniques more power. The great force that a practitioner of the internal martial arts can deliver in his or her palm strike or punch is because of the explosive power of the Jin.

While normal physical strength comes from the expansion and contraction of the muscles, Jin comes more from the development of an elastic quality in the tendons, ligaments, and sinews, and can be likened to the power of a spring being continuously coiled and released.

The explosive power of Jin can be likened to the whole-body action of a man wielding an axe rather than a hammer.

The tendons in the body are always kept slightly flexed. It is this that attracts the Qi to them so they can be nourished and grow. The tendons wrap around the bones and form a latticework throughout the body. The tendons go from the tips of the fingers to the tips of the toes and the top of the head. Real Jin is when the tendons, sinews, and ligaments combine with the acupuncture meridians to create an internal structure in the body that feels like flexible steel cable.

The movements of people who cannot let go of their muscle tension are like dead, brittle branches that would break were the wind to blow. Others unfortunately are completely relaxed in both their muscles and tendons, and their movements are like blades of limp grass that bend, and stay bent, in the wind. To be balanced we don't want to be too Yang (hard) or too Yin (soft). We want to be flexible and resilient like young bamboo so, when the wind blows, we bend and then spring back.

For general health Jin adds a spring to one's step and develops a noticeable vitality to the body. As we get older, we can sustain higher energy levels, and we can stay flexible and active because we have developed our Jin. Inevitably as a person acquires more Qi and more Jin, their body resistance gets stronger, their overall vitality increases, and their chances of a long life in good health improve.

FA JIN: AN EXPLOSIVE RELEASE OF INTERNAL FORCE

Fa jin is at the highest level of internal martial arts training. It is an advanced technique that is usually kept so secret that it is possible that the majority of practitioners are not aware of it. The old Masters often hinted at it, but never explained it in great detail, so it was often never grasped by the students. To be able to use internal martial arts effectively for self-defense, and to be able to get the highest level of health benefit, we need to be doing Fa jin in almost all aspects of our training.

Fa means "to release," and jin means "internal force." Fa jin, then, is an "explosive release of internal force." A lot of the power in a Fa jin movement comes from the elastic power of tendons, ligaments, and the sinews in the whole body. To understand this, compare the action to a bow firing an arrow. Although it is the arrow which inflicts the damage, it is in itself powerless. The arrow needs the elastic force of the archer's bow to make it effective. In the same way, the fist needs the Jin of the body behind it to make its strike effective.

A vigorous shake of the waist is one of the main ways of initiating a Fa jin. This shake travels through the whole body, and by the time it reaches the hands and feet, the force is so concentrated that the punch or kick has incredible power.

Fa jin is a shaking movement done with the whole body, and in combat a strike can be done with the fists and feet, knees, elbows, shoulders, and head. Whatever part of our body is closest becomes the best weapon to strike a target area.

1. Hands held in preparation at the beginning of this fluid movement

2. The weight is moved onto the front leg

3. The waist turns to the left and the right fist is thrown forward

4. The right fist continues its movement into a punch

The concentrated, shaking force of the Fa jin is similar in many ways to the cracking of a bullwhip. The movement of the handle is not that fast, but by the time the flowing force has reached the end of the whip, it is faster than the speed of sound. The "cracking" sound one gets from cracking a bull whip is created because the end of the whip is breaking the sound barrier and making a small sonic boom. Part of the supersonic flicking of the tail of the whip is caused by the pull-back on the handle of the whip. The usual whip handle motion is up and down, and this is followed by another upward movement. This creates a wave that flows along the whip and causes the tip of it to flick and crack.

The action of the body in a Fa jin strike is the same. The waist turns out and back and out again. This waist shake sends a wave of Qi flowing along the body and out to the hands which flick and snap. A Fa jin move is not just a fast move, it is an explosive, shaking, whole body movement, just like a sneeze.

The slow movements of the internal martial arts are used to build up Qi, and the Fa jin explosive movements are used to release the excess. Slow movements without Fa jin are like Yin without Yang: unbalanced. To practice the forms of the internal martial arts slowly or fast, but not explosively, would be like a person saying that they do archery, but only draw the bow and never release the arrow!

From a health point of view, Fa jin can be likened to boiling a pot of water. Just as steam pressure builds up inside the pot and will crack the sides unless the lid is lifted to let off some steam, so a

5. Once the punch is complete, the waist recoils back to the right, bringing the fist back

6. The weight returns to the right leg

7. The recoil action of the waist causes the left hand to be thrown forward for another strike

The push power for the Fa jin comes from the back leg, which turns and the weight goes forward onto the left leg, which throws the right hand forward with a hammer hand punch.

The recoil to this movement brings the weight back onto the right leg; the waist also turns back to the right, and the left hand is thrown forward for another strike.

person who has generated too much Qi could overheat and burn themselves out.

With the above idea, the body is the pot, the water is the body fluids (blood, nutrient substances, essence, and hormones), and the steam is the Qi (energetic activity). One of the main reasons that we stand still and store the Qi in the Lower Dan Dien at the end of every training session is so the steam can cool down and condense back into water to replenish the system.

For self-defense we use Fa jin when attacking the acupuncture points on the opponent's body. The most advanced type of Fa jin is called the Vibrating Palm Fa jin and this is also the tool for applying the most advanced Qi healing techniques to a patient. The palms are placed over the appropriate acupuncture points, and, using the Vibrating Palm Fa jin, Qi is transmitted to the patient. There is virtually no visible external body movements, but internally the palms of the hands are vibrate as they emit Qi. The Vibrating Palm Fa jin can be used for healing or point striking, depending on the circumstances and the intention that one gives to the Qi energy.

The healing benefit of incorporating Fa jin into training is that through it, stagnant Qi is loosened and shaken from the body. Most internal martial arts styles only introduce Fa jin at an advanced stage of training, but without it development is limited and the ability to heal others will never reach the highest level.

The healing benefits of the Vibrating Palm Fa jin are achieved by Qi passing from practitioner to patient.

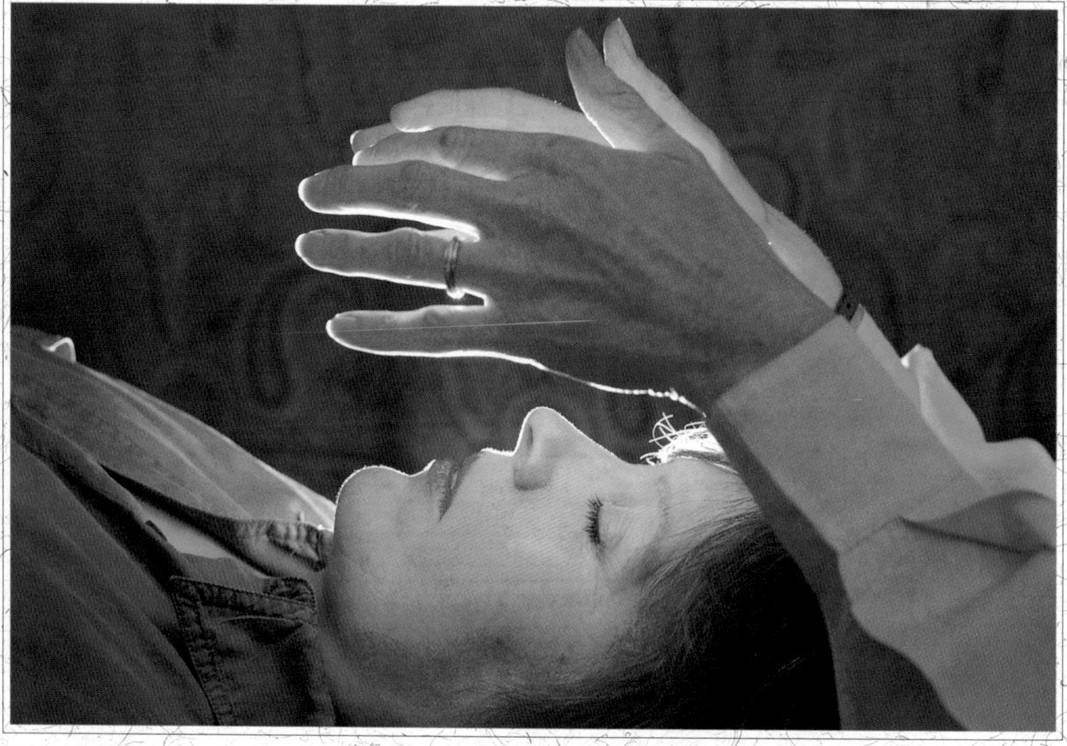

The Yellow Emperor, author of the classic text on Chinese Medicine upon which the foundation of the internal martial arts is based.

Taijiquan

YIN YANG FIST

THE CHINESE INTERNAL martial art of Taijiquan is the most popular in the world. Most people today practice it for the great health benefits it has to offer, and as a process for self and spiritual development, rather than for its self-defense applications. However, for those who know how to use it well, Taijiquan is one of the most effective and devastating martial art styles ever invented.

There are many different styles of Taijiquan, each with slightly different forms, but they all share the same principles, in that the movements should always be continuous, smooth, circular, and flowing. When Taijiquan is practiced just for its health benefits, the slower the movement, the greater the benefit. A medium speed strengthens the physical body, while a slow speed benefits the flow of Qi. A very slow speed (so slow that you cannot feel yourself move) heals the spirit.

When Taijiquan is practiced for its self-defense aspects, there are many explosive Fa jin movements. Indeed, at the highest level of self-healing and self-defense every move becomes a Fa jin.

In addition to the single-person empty-handed forms for which Taijiquan is most famous, there are also many two-person training systems, including

Pushing Hands is a two person training exercise to develop balance, timing, and coordination.

The spine is always straight and vertical

Strength and stability is needed on the standing leg

The leg is straightened to get full power into the kick

In addition to empty-hand forms, Taijiquan has weapons forms. This sequence demonstrates a move from the Walking Stick form.

Pushing Hands, Da Lu, and Lung Har Quan (Taiji Dragon Prawn Boxing). The Old Yang style of Taijiquan also has a large two-person fighting set called the San Sau, which is very forceful and invigorating. The New Yang style of Taijiquan has a simplified version of this which is more gentle.

Taijiquan also has weapons forms, including the Sword and Dagger form, the Single Saber and Double Saber forms, the Short Stick form, the Staff form, and the Spear form. There is also a Taijiquan Walking Stick form that is now becoming very popular.

For many years in the West it was believed that Taijiquan was only of benefit to the old or infirm. It is now realized that it is good for people of all ages. Instead of using Taijiquan just as a way of recovering from ill health, if training is started early, illness in old age can be prevented.

In Taijiquan the movements are dynamic and resilient and help develop an attitude of confidence and decisiveness. This positive attitude is not only good for building self-confidence, but has also been shown to boost the immune system and so improve the body's resistance to illness and improve general health. This is because by building a strong Fighting Spirit into the self-defense aspects of our Taijiquan training, we simultaneously cultivate a stronger internal defensive system that will combat disease more effectively.

As a soft style Taijiquan promotes an increase in the circulation of blood and Qi energy around the body, which in turn produces a feeling of relaxation and calm. These aspects of Taijiquan have made it attractive to many people as a way of releasing stress.

Taijiquan also develops flexibility as well as balance

WHAT DOES "TAIJIQUAN" MEAN?

Taiji is the name of the Yin Yang symbol pictured below, and quan literally translates as "fist," but also carries the meaning of "martial art." Together Taijiquan means a fighting system based on the principles of Yin and Yang.

The principle idea behind the Yin and Yang theory is that there should be a dynamic balance in all things at all levels. The aim of Taijiquan is to achieve this balance in energy, body, mind, emotions, and spirit.

Taijiquan practitioners strive for the ultimate balance of Yin and Yang, as embodied in the Taiji symbol.

By practicing Taijiquan, people with poor health are made stronger and those with a tendency to be hyperactive become more at ease. People who feel anxious become more confident and those who have an angry temperament feel calmed. Eventually everyone who practices Taijiquan develops a happy, healing feeling.

THE HISTORY AND CLASSICS OF TAIJIQUAN

Taijiquan is a combination of healing and martial arts techniques developed in China in the thirteenth century and now written down in the *Classics of Taijiquan*.

Chang San feng

It is unlikely that Taijiquan is the creation of just one person. It was most probably created over a long period of time and has been influenced by many generations of dedicated martial artists.

However, the person regarded by the majority of researchers to be its originator is Chang San feng (born 1270 A.D.).

Chang San feng developed the methods of Taijiquan after a twenty-year period of study, half of which was spent in the Shaolin monastery.

He spent ten years learning many different Qigong healing techniques and martial arts from the Buddhist monks of the Shaolin Temple who developed Kung Fu.

He then spent at least another ten years learning more Qigong healing techniques and martial arts on Wudang Mountain from the Daoist hermits who lived there.

He created Taijiquan by combining the best principles of the martial arts styles and Qigong self-healing techniques from both places. He was a great fighter and is reputed to have killed over 100 people in hand to hand combat during his life. He achieved an incredibly high level of expertise and lived to be over 100 years old, while still

Wudang Mountain where Chang San feng spent ten years learning the Qigong healing techniques and martial arts on which he was to base Taijiquan.

The Buddhist stupas of the Shaolin monastery; each one contains a relic from a monk who worshiped there.

maintaining great physical power and spiritual force. Legend says that he didn't die, but transformed himself into pure spirit and flew away.

Chang San feng wrote down some of his methods, which have been handed down from generation to generation. Today they form part of the *Classics of Taijiquan*, a collection of methods and principles from various practitioners, which were handed down orally over the centuries and later written down. Here is a translation of a small part of his works:

> *The body must move as a single unit*
> *at one with the Breath, Qi, and Spirit.*
>
> *The Rooting of the feet, the strength*
> *of the legs,*
> *and the power of the waist all manifest*
> *in the hands.*
> *The whole body is connected moving as one.*
> *Our movement is guided by our Intention.*
>
> *Taijiquan is like the great river rolling*
> *on unceasingly.*
>
> CHANG SAN FENG

Wang Tsung yueh

During the eighteenth century, Taijiquan was eventually passed down to Wang Tsung yueh, whose methods have also now become part of the *Classics of Taijiquan*. Here are some extracts from his works (my translation):

> *Yin and Yang continually transform*
> *within each move;*
> *without this balance the Qi stagnates.*
>
> *Allow the Qi to gather in the*
> *Lower Dan Dien;*
> *from long practice one develops Jin.*
>
> *Pursue the opponent and move*
> *as he moves;*
> *know his intention while concealing yours.*
>
> *To be an unequaled fighter results*
> *from this.*
>
> WANG TSUNG YUEH

極

THE FAMILY STYLES OF TAIJIQUAN

The main branches of Taijiquan that exist today of the family styles of the Yang, the Wu, and the Chen. Each family claims to have created the true Taijiquan: the truth is probably found in a combination of all three versions.

Chen Fake (1887–1957) bought Taijiquan to Beijing in 1928.

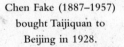

Yang Lu Chan (1799–1872) creator of the Old Yang Style of Taijiquan.

The Chen Family Style

The inheritor of Wang Tsung yueh' s Taijiquan system was Chiang Fa, who, it is argued, then taught it to the Chen family. The Chen family, however, say it was not this outsider but one of their own ancestors, Chen Wang ting, who created Taijiquan in the seventeenth century. They claim that Chen Chang xing (1771-1853) inherited the system and that his great-grandson Chen Fake (1887-1957) brought the Chen family style of Taijiquan to Beijing and public attention in 1928.

We will never know for sure how it got there, but Taijiquan is still practiced today in the Chen family village, Chen Cia Kou, in Honan province. It should be noted that the Shaolin Temple is relatively close to the Chen family village, and it is argued that this proximity may well have directly influenced the Chen style of Taijiquan.

The Yang Family Style

The Yang family claim that it was Yang Lu chan (1799-1872) who created the system. After completing his training in the fighting systems of the Shaolin Temple, he then learned Taijiquan from another group of martial artists who lived on Wudang Mountain. This group's lineage went all the way back to Chang San feng.

Yang Lu chan then formulated his own version of Taijiquan, which is today called the Old Yang style of Taijiquan. (This is because his name was Yang and has nothing to do with the central concept of Yin and Yang).

Yang Cheng fou, whose style of Taijiquan is the most widely practiced today.

He then set out to find a better fighter than himself, and whenever he heard of a martial artist in the area where he was traveling, he would challenge them. Often he fought with several people at once but was never beaten.

It is said that he visited the Chen family village, and after defeating some of their best fighters, he explained some of his theories to them, which they went on to incorporate into their family style, to make it into Taijiquan. Another account says the Chen family fighters were defeated only because Yang was using skills he had learned from them at an earlier time. Today some people say the Yang style comes from the Chen style, and others say they influenced each other but are clearly different styles. We will never know the truth.

Yang Jiang hou, one of the members of the Yang family of practitioners.

Eventually Yang Lu chan's reputation was so great that when he arrived in Beijing he was asked to be Instructor Of The Royal Guard, where he became known as Yang of No Equal.

He taught his Old Yang style to his son Yang Jian hou (1839-1917) and his grandson Yang Shao hu (1862-1930), who went on to teach it to his second cousin Chang Yiu chun (1899-1986) who, in turn, taught it to my own teacher Erle Montaigue. However, it is the simplified version known as the New Yang style, developed by Yang Chen fu (1883-1936), Yang Shao hu's brother, which is now probably the most widely practiced style of Taijiquan today.

The Wu Family Style

The second most widely practiced style of Taijiquan, after the Yang style, is probably the Wu style. Wu Chien chuan (1870-1942) who learned it from Wu Quan you (1834-1902), who learned from Yang Pan hou (1837-1892), the brother of Yang Jiang hou (1839-1917). There is also a less well-known Wu style created by Wu Yu hsiang (1812-1880). He was a student of Yang Lu chan and Chen Ching ping, so this Wu style was born out of a combination of the Chen and Yang styles.

Wu Yu hsiang's style was passed on to Hao Weiz heng (1849-1920) and Sun Luc tang (1861-1932). Only a few people today practice the Sun and Hao styles of Taijiquan.

Wu Yu hsiang has also contributed to the *Classics Of Taijiquan*. Here are some extracts of some of his writings (my translation):

The body follows the Qi which
follows the Intention,
If the movement is flowing we can
develop Jin.

Jin is generated in the spine like
drawing a bow,
Fa jin is like the release of an arrow.

Our form is dynamic like a falcon about
to seize a rabbit,
Our Spirit is sharp like a cat about
to catch a rat.

Be as stable as a mountain and flow
like the great river.

WU YU HSIANG

THE ANIMAL QUALITIES OF TAIJIQUAN

In the *Classics of Taijiquan* many of the names of the movements make reference to animals: for example, the Crane Cools Its Wings; Monkey Strike; Snake Spitting Venom; Grasping The Sparrow's Tail; Draw The Bow To Shoot The Tiger.

This is not only because some of the movements express the characteristics of certain animals and their movements, but also because different animals have different qualities that we want to develop within ourselves. For example, Taijiquan training will give us the strong bones of a tiger, the excellent vision of a bird of prey, and the lightning speed of a striking snake.

The way we move in Taijiquan finds many parallels with the animal world. We rotate and twist the whole body continuously like a snake. When one part moves, the whole of the body

DRAW THE BOW TO SHOOT THE TIGER

CRANE COOLS ITS WINGS

MONKEY STRIKE

moves. When we stand on one leg, we need the same strength, balance, and stability as a stork, and our hands should move like the wings of a bird.

In self-defense our impact with the opponent should have the same force as a bird of prey at the end of its power dive, impacting with its victim. We should step like a tiger stalking its prey, feeling the ground before it carefully puts its foot down, and we should be attentive like a cat about to pounce on a mouse, coiled and ready to spring. And we should strike like the cat pouncing on the mouse, with extended fingers (like a cat's claws) and an arched back.

If we watch a cat carefully, we can see that when they curl up to go to sleep they touch their tails to their noses. It is in this observed behavior that we can see the universal nature of the Internal Qigong exercise known as The Small Circulation of Qi (see page 29).

Grasping the Sparrow's Tail

Snake Spitting Venom

TAIJIQUAN POSTURE

In Taijiquan great emphasis is placed on correct posture. This is to ensure that Qi flow is strong and unimpeded, and that the body provides a firm structure for the self-defense applications.

The feet should claw the ground to help develop Rooting (see page 26). This also activates the first point on the Kidney Meridian (K-1), through which Qi energy can be exchanged with the earth, to heal ourselves and others, and to make a deeper spiritual connection with nature.

Knees should be kept slightly bent to strengthen the legs by making them support the full body weight, and also lower the center of gravity. This is important as the balance we achieve by having a lower center of gravity helps us maintain both emotional and mental balance.

The spine should be kept straight, and this can be achieved by imagining a string pulling up at the back of the head. To straighten the lower spine, the coccyx should tilted forward under the torso - this should happen naturally when the knees are bent.

If the spine is straight while we perform the rotating and spiraling movements of Taijiquan, then its flexibility is increased. Furthermore, this increases the flow of spinal fluid and improves the functioning of the spinal nerves. Qi can ascend up the center of the spine, through the Governing Meridian, to the head on its journey through the Small Circulation of Qi (see page 29). By keeping the spine healthy in this way, we reduce the possibility of developing lumbago, sciatica, prolapsed disks, and other back problems.

The tongue should be placed on the roof of the mouth to complete the circuit of the Small Circulation of Qi and to bring it back down into the belly. The position of the tongue should be as if we are saying the letter L. If we did not connect the tongue, then energy would accumulate in the head. It is important that excess energy is never left in the head, because the hard bone of the skull cannot expand to take the pressure. This trapped Qi will cause headaches and excessive mental activity. It is vital we connect the tongue and bring the Qi down to the belly. It should not be left in the chest

The body should be vertically aligned between the crown and Kidney One

Shoulders are dropped slightly forward and should be relaxed

Knees should not be bent further than the end of the toes

Correct posture is essential to the flow of Qi. Although there are many things to remember, with practice this will come naturally.

because, again, the ribcage cannot expand enough to take the excess Qi. If it is left here, it will cause discomfort.

Only by bringing the Qi down to the Lower Dan Dien (see page 34) can we be balanced and stable. The belly is soft and can expand to accommodate excess Qi and is the safest place to store energy. Also, if at any time saliva accumulates in the mouth, this should be swallowed. This helps carry the Qi down into the belly. The only time the tongue does not touch the roof of the mouth at all is during a Fa jin explosive move accompanied by a shout, or during a special Qigong exercise.

The shoulders should be allowed to relax and sink down, dropped slightly forward. This stops the shoulders, neck, and upper back from becoming tense and allows the Qi to sink into the belly. Keeping the shoulders high and tense is a bad habit that can increase mental tension. By relaxing them down and forward, we can release both mental and physical tension.

Elbows should remain below shoulder level, as it is easier for the shoulders to relax. There should always be a space under the armpits about the size of a fist, so that the energy can flow freely through the shoulder joints and down the arms.

Occasionally in some of the self-defense applications, the arms do lock out. However, most of the time the arms always maintain a circular shape, as if hugging a large tree. The arms should not be bent too much at the elbows, because this will reduce the flow of Qi. If we imagine that Qi flowing through the arms is like water through a hose, then a bent elbow is like a bend in the hose, stopping the water from flowing.

The circular shape of the arms not only refers to each of the arms individually, but also to the shape which both of them form together. This is achieved by stretching the arms forward until you feel them connect across the upper back, forming, horizontally, the shape of a horseshoe.

The Dragon's Mouth promotes the flow of Qi.

The hands should be slightly flexed as if reaching out to grab someone. This creates a slight flex in the tendons of the hands, but there is, of course, no tension in the muscles. The flex draws the Qi down the meridians that correspond to the tendons, so we feel a fullness in our fingertips. The fingers should not be touching each other. The hands are held concave so that we can hold the Qi in the palm. This hand posture activates the eighth point on the Pericardium Meridian. This point is used to emit Qi for both the martial arts and the healing techniques.

The thumb should be held away from the other fingers. The weblike piece of skin between the index finger and thumb should be stretched straight. This creates what is called the Dragon's Mouth, and the clawlike shape of the hands increases the flow of Qi not just in the hands but in the whole body.

For self-defense applications, the fingers should be flexed and extended so they develop strength due to the increased Qi flow. Eventually, they become like steel daggers and can be used as an effective weapon with which to stab an opponent. Powerful hands and fingers that can emit a concentrated flow of Qi also increase healing capabilities when applying acupressure massage.

THE PRINCIPLES OF TAIJIQUAN

All Taijiquan movements should be circular and spiraling. This natural, fluid movement is both Yin and Yang. Yin is centripetal, spiraling inward, while Yang is centrifugal, spiraling outward. The circular movement comes from the vigorous waist rotation and helps the blood and Qi circulation, without straining the heart. Every Taijiquan move is circular, even the punches have a slight corkscrew action. When practiced slowly, the movements are like a whirlpool; when practiced fast, like a whirlwind. When we execute a series of Fa jin explosive movements, they should become a cyclone of spiraling power, calm in our center, but outwardly manifesting an unstoppable force.

The spiraling and twisting movements of the torso and the subtle rotations of all the joints make the whole body flow like a great river. When Taijiquan is practiced this way, the powerful energy can be felt spiraling up and down, around the arms, legs, and torso. The rotating and twisting of the waist massages all the internal organs increasing Qi. The internal organs are reservoirs for the body's energy, and Taijiquan movements encourage Qi to flow from them through the body's meridian system (see page 29), like water flowing from a great reservoir down to a river.

The centrifugal and centripetal waist power is also used with kicks and punches, and can generate a very powerful strike. The waist turns back and forth, and the legs or arms are thrown out and back.

The waist turns to the right with the weight going slightly onto the right leg

The right hand turns palm down and moves down, while the left hand moves palm up, moving upward inside the right wrist

The waist starts to move to the left and the weight begins to go onto the left leg

A technique used to develop centrifugal and centripetal waist power is to go through the whole form very slowly and move the waist a quarter of a second before the rest of the body moves. Once this principle has been grasped and internalized, then the hands, feet, and waist all appear to move at the same time.

If our external movements are calm, smooth, and flowing, then internally our Qi will flow smoothly throughout our body, balancing and healing us, producing mental and emotioal stability and calm and a state of well-being.

When practicing Taijiquan, it is important to let go of unnecessary tensions both in the body and in the mind, and to be relaxed and sunk into the Taijiquan posture. Letting go of physical tension makes it easier to let go of mental tension, which in turn allows us to let go of physical tension, and so on. Hand-eye coordination and response speed are also improved when we are relaxed.

Tense muscles are also counterproductive in self-defense. When we strike, we need to extend the arm or leg, and muscle contraction or tension will restrict this movement. If we relax, the arm or leg can be extended smoothly and freely.

All Taijiquan is done with mental intention, not muscle tension. Even at the point of impact, there is no muscle tension. When we are relaxed, our center of gravity becomes lower and lower, so that physically and mentally we are more stable and balanced. This is good both for self-defense and in everyday life.

Both hands turn over as one turns the body

The waist is now turned to the left, and the weight has moved farther onto the left leg. The left hand moves palm down and the right hand moves palm up. To complete the movement, turn the waist to the right, moving the weight to the right leg and repeating the sequence.

The Taijiquan sequence, Waving Hands like Clouds, is said to heal problems with the stomach and digestive system. When practiced correctly, the hands feel as light as clouds.

THE YIN YANG CHANGES OF TAIJIQUAN

Taijiquan means "Yin Yang Fist" (see page 43). It is a system based around the concept of keeping Yin and Yang in harmonious balance at all times and at all levels.

In the legs the Yin Yang balance is achieved by storing and releasing internal power from leg to leg, like springs compressing and releasing. The other Yin Yang change is in the shift of body weight from leg to leg.

In the waist the Yin Yang change is achieved by the waist turning from side to side. The centrifugal and centripetal waist power is driven by pushing the legs. When the leg pushes, the waist turns, and the hand is thrown out to hit the target. We do not punch through the target, nor do we punch and stop on impact. We are using centrifugal Yang energy and centripetal Yin energy, so we punch and pull back so that there is a deep, penetrating percussive blow transmitted to the opponent. This out-and-back Yin Yang waist recoil action is the power supply for Fa jin.

In Taijiquan the practitioner aims to achieve a perfect balance of Yin and Yang.

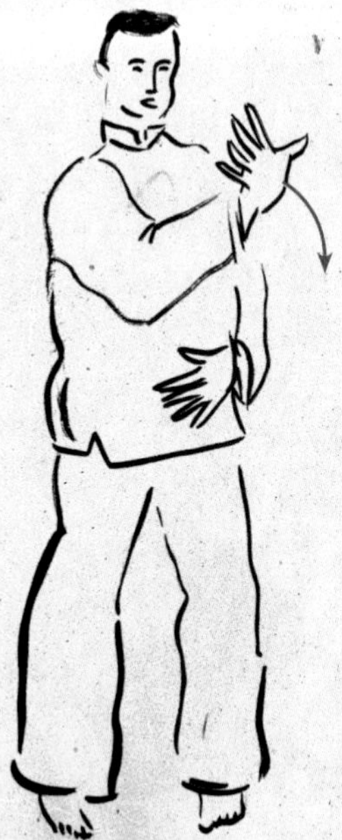

The movement of the wrist is directly connected to the movement of energy in the Lower Dan Dien. This gives the practitioner's strikes great power for self-defense and helps circulate the energy for self-healing

The most advanced Yin Yang change is in the hands. This change is more of a continual flow, from a Yang palm to a Yin palm. Neither ever reaches its maximum, and is always in a state of transformation. This flowing change is as if the hands were trailing through water, or as if the movement of the hands were like the wings of a bird.

Of course, in Taijiquan nothing is linear, and because we are always turning, rotating, and twisting, the hands and wrists do not move horizontally or vertically, but rather in Yin inward spirals and Yang outward spirals.

The Yin Yang hand changes store and release Qi. As one's ability develops, a very powerful Qi density builds up within and around the hands, which feels very much like a hot electromagnetic force. This Qi can be used positively to heal others by placing the hands on the part of the body that needs healing.

With enough practice, this Qi field builds up around the whole body, and excess Qi radiates out into the whole world. The more people who reach this happy stage, the brighter the world in which we live will be.

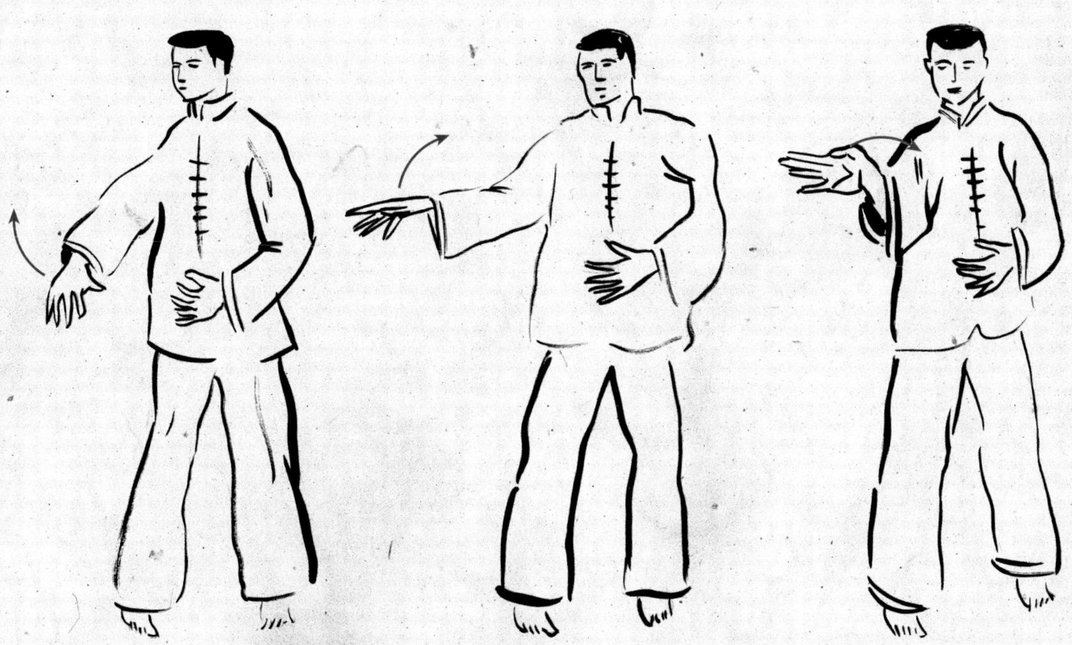

For the Taijiquan Yin Yang hand to work correctly, the wrist must be relaxed so that the hand follows the forearm as if it is trailing through water

TAIJIQUAN WEAPONS

Taijiquan has several weapons forms: the Long Sword and Dagger form; the Single Saber and Double Saber forms; the Short Stick form; the Staff form; the Spear form, and the Walking Stick form. (The latter is a very good form for old people living in a dangerous place to know, as it means they have a weapon with which to defend themselves which is legal and does not attract attention).

The weapons forms are usually taught after the empty-hand forms have been learned. In the Long Sword and Dagger form, the sword is held in the right hand and the dagger in the left hand. Most people today, however, no longer use the dagger, and the left hand remains empty. The Double Sabre form is particularly beneficial because it exercises both sides of the body equally. The other weapons forms are learned first with the weapon in the right hand, and then with the weapon in the left hand.

Some people say that the Single Saber form was the first weapons form, the saber being a variation on the machete, a widely used and common agricultural tool in Asia, and as such should be learned first. Other people say that the Short Stick form was the first form, because the short stick was man's

The Taijiquan Staff form develops the ability to channel energy beyond the body.

To the practitioner the staff feels like an extra limb

As well as speed and strength, flexibility is also developed

The intention of the practitioner reaches right to the tip of the blade
The circular movement of both sabers comes from the waist rotation

The Taijiquan Saber form allows the practitioner to develop great strength and fluid movement.

The Taijiquan Double Saber form balances and strengthens both sides of the body and develops symmetrical coordination.

first tool, and as such this form should be learned first. People and circumstances vary widely, so there is no fixed format, but in general the usual order in which the weapons are taught is the short single weapons first: Short Stick, Walking Stick, and Single Saber. The double weapons forms should then follow: Double Sabre and Sword and Dagger. Finally the long weapons forms should be learned: Staff and Spear.

Whatever the form, however, a weapon should always feel as if it is a part of us, like an extra limb, and the Qi that emanates from us should extend to the end of the weapon. All the weapons forms at an advanced level contain Fa jin. It is vitally important that the wooden weapons are made of rattan, which is flexible, and not hard wood which is too stiff. This is so that the shaking, vibrating energy can flow down to the end of the weapon. If the wooden weapon is hard and stiff, the shaking Qi could get trapped in the body and cause damage.

When we practice the weapons forms, we are relaxed. The weight of the weapon forces the body to release more Qi to support the extra weight we are holding, and more Qi flowing around the body results in a greater healing benefit.

TAIJIQUAN FIGHTING STRATEGY

Practitioners of the internal martial art of Taijiquan are practicing to build themselves up rather than to defeat others. Confrontation is avoided, and the first strategy is always to try to diffuse trouble rather than encourage it.

However, when there is no other option, the Taijiquan fighting strategy is to counterattack your opponent simultaneously, or as your opponent

A Taijiquan Application

The Taijiquan response to an opponent's attack is to counterattack forward immediately with a series of Fa jin movements.

These movements can be practiced against an imaginary opponent, or slowly as a moving meditation sequence, to get an idea of what the style feels like.

1. The opponent steps in with the right foot and executes a straight, right punch to the head of the Taijiquan practitioner.

2. The Taijiquan practitioner responds with the movements of Double Right Palm Circle, stepping with his left foot to the outside of the attacker's right arm, and attacking with his right heel palm just above the elbow of the opponent's right arm. The Taijiquan practitioner simultaneously executes a palm strike with his left hand to the opponent's jaw. This movement of the hands circling up and to the right is as a result of a vigorous turn of the waist to the right.

moves to attack you using a series of continuous explosive Fa jin attacking movements.

The most common counterattack in Taijiquan is to move straight toward the oncoming opponent, simultaneously attacking their attacking limb - the arm in the case of a punch, the leg in the case of a kick - and at the same time attacking the neck, head, or torso.

3. The Taijiquan practitioner follows through with Inspection of Horse's Mouth, by turning his waist to the left causing his left palm to push the opponent's right arm down and his fingers on his right hand to strike into the opponent's neck.

Baguazhang

EIGHT TRIAGRAM PALM

BAGUAZHANG (Pa Kwa Chang) means "Eight Triagram Palm." It is very popular in mainland China, and over 40 books have been published there on it. In this soft style the hands are kept open, and the palms are used for striking the opponent. Hence, its name ends with the word zhang which means "palm" rather than quan which means "fist" - as in Taijiquan (Yin Yang Fist) or Xingyiquan (Form Intention Fist). Ba gua translates literally as "Eight Triagrams."

Baguazhang is not as soft as Taijiquan, but it is softer than Xingyiquan. It has separate circular forms and also a linear form. Taijiquan forms have both linear and circular aspects within them, and Xingyiquan has only linear forms.

Although there are over 20 different styles of Baguazhang, they are all different interpretations of the same basic principles, and all contain the eight basic shapes in the way the hand (palm) is held. These are known as the Eight Palm Changes.

These movements involve blocks, kicks, trips, strikes, and breaking techniques that are practiced in a continuous way while walking first in a clockwise circle, and then in an a counterclockwise circle. This circle is the outside edge of the Yin Yang diagram, and it is sectioned into the Eight Triagrams of The Yi jing (*Book of Changes* - see page14). Some styles of Baguazhang have additional palm changes named after animals. Others have linear forms, although they are not as familiar to people as the Bagua Circle Walking forms.

The Eight Palm Changes of Baguazhang (see page 68) are relatively straightforward at a basic level. However, they have an unlimited number of variations and applications, and it takes many years to grasp the more advanced aspects.

There are eight shapes in which the palm is held in Baguazhang.

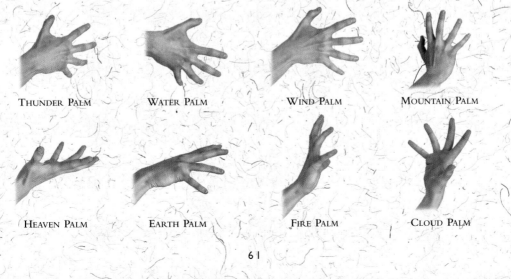

THUNDER PALM

WATER PALM

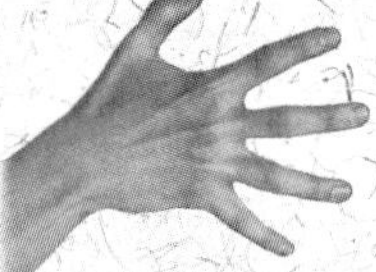
WIND PALM

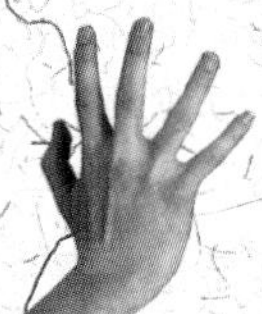
MOUNTAIN PALM

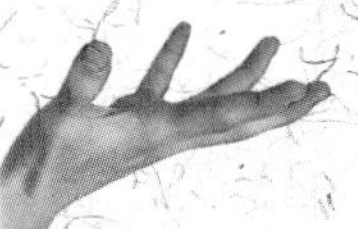
HEAVEN PALM

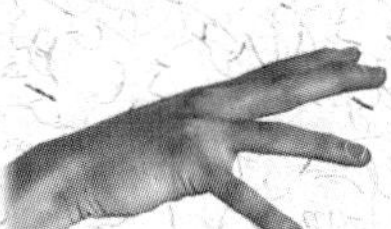
EARTH PALM

FIRE PALM

CLOUD PALM

BAGUAZHANG AND LONGEVITY

Baguazhang is one of the great internal martial arts of China. It is famous not only for the great fighting skills of its practitioners, but also for the great longevity it can confer on them. The best example of this is Master Li Ching yuan (1678–1928) who lived to the age of 250 years.

Master Li Ching yuan studied with the Daoists on Emei Mountain in Sichuan province and attained great longevity through his natural lifestyle, good diet, and practice of Qigong techniques combined with Baguazhang training.

It is unlikely that a person living in a modern city with its pollution and stress could match this lifespan. However, virtually all the great Baguazhang Masters reached grand old ages in good health. The swirling, rotating, and twisting movements of Baguazhang squeeze out the stagnant Qi from the body and invigorate the circulation of good, healing Qi. If practiced regularly this internal martial art will extend one's life so that old age can be enjoyed in good health.

Practicing Baguazhang led Master Li Chung yuan to live to the age of 250.

HISTORY OF BAGUAZHANG

It is unclear exactly when or where in China Baguazhang was created, although its origins are thought to be many hundreds of years old. The first written accounts of Baguazhang date back to the Qing dynasty (A.D. 1644–1912).

The first recognized Baguazhang Master was Dong Meng lin. Other martial artists held him in high esteem for his chivalrous behavior and his high level of ability. He was also known as The Yellow Cape Daoist because he was as strong and steady as the earth, (in Daoism the color yellow is associated with earth).

Dong Meng lin taught his system to three main students in the Kianasu Mountains. The most famous of these was Dong Hai chuan (A.D. 1797-1882) from Hebei province.

Dong Hai chuan is widely recognized because he had many students and was instrumental in spreading the art. His best student was Cheng Ting hua, also of Hebei province, who fought and died during the opium war of 1900.

In the West the best–known student of Cheng Ting hua was Sun Luc Tang (1860–1932). His books, *The Study of Bagua Fist* (1916) and *The Study of Bagua Sword* (1925), are still regarded today as essential reference works. Sun Luc tang was not only an expert in Baguazhang, but also in Taijiquan and Xingyiquan. He was recognized as a great weapons fighter in the Staff and the Sword forms.

All the different students of Dong Meng lin and Dong Hai chuan went on to open their own schools of Baguazhang, and this has resulted in many different variations today. There is the Dragon Shape Style of Baguazhang, the Yin Style of Bagua, the Swimming Body Walking Style of Baguazhang, theLinking Palms Bagua, the Nine Palace Three Coiling Palms Baguazhang, the Yin Yang Eight Coiling Palms, and the Nine Dragon Eight Triagram Palm Style, as well as Wudang and Emei Mountain styles.

The Emei Mountains in Sichuan province, one of the centers of Daoism and of Baguazhang.

The Yi jing is an expression of the common origins and characteristics of every living thing on the earth and their relationship with the universe.

THE YI JING IN BAGUAZHANG

The foundation of the art of Baguazhang, the Eight Palm Changes, are based on the Eight Triagrams of one of the earliest Chinese philosophical work, The Yi jing, commonly known as the *Book of Changes*. Different schools of Baguazhang make different correspondences between the Eight Palm Changes and The Eight Triagrams. However, they all acknowledge that the greatness of the art is in its ability to change and adapt to circumstances.

This is the nature of The Yi jing: it is a profound work of insight that is over 4,000 years old and contains within it the principles that explain the changing nature of life.

THE HISTORY OF THE YI JING

The Yi jing is thought to have been originated by Fu Xi, one of China's first emperors, in 2852 B.C. It was further classified and organized by Wen Wang, the first ruler of the state of Zhou in 1122 B.C.

Wen Wang said that Fu Xi had been able to formulate The Yi jing because he had spent a lifetime observing the Qi of the heavens in the behavior of the sun, moon, and stars, and all the various forms that nature took on earth. He studied the behavior of animals and people, the changing of the weather and the seasons. His studies revealed patterns and repetitions that were common to all phenomena, and Fu Xi interpreted these patterns and created a diagram that expressed them all. That diagram is the Eight Triagrams of The Yi jing.

The Eight Triagrams of the Yi jing laid out in the arrangement drawn up by Fu Xi.

THE MEANING OF THE EIGHT TRIAGRAMS OF THE YI JING

A Triagram is a three-line diagram made up of broken and continuous lines. A continuous line symbolizes Yang; a broken line symbolizes Yin. The Eight Triagrams (three-line diagrams) show all the possible combinations for Yin and Yang.

For example, the triagram Kan has just one Yang line between two Yin lines. This is like the white (Yang) dot in the dark Yin half of the Taiji diagram. Similarly, the triagram Li has one Yin line between two Yang lines, and is like the dark (Yin) dot within the bright Yang half of the Taiji diagram. The number of Yin lines increases and the number of Yang decreases as one descends down one side of the Taiji diagram and then this process is reversed as one ascends up the other side. Thus the triagrams reflect the waxing and waning of Yin and Yang.

The eight different triagrams combine together in pairs to make sixty-four hexagrams, each corresponding to an explanation in The Yi jing. These can be used as a means of divination, to analyze cause and effect, and, by observing the pattern that is developing, to deduce the possible future outcome. In the agricultural communities of ancient China, it was applied to the planting and harvesting of crops in relation to the waxing and

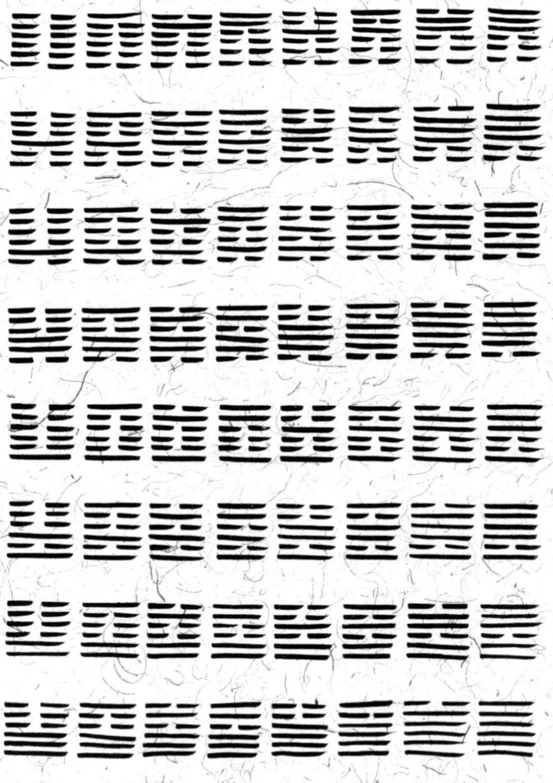

The eight triagrams can be combined to form sixty-four hexagrams.

Maintaining continual Qi circulation is vital to martial power. Its pattern of flow may be based upon the Eight Triagrams.

QIAN

Qi will circulate if the spine is straight and stretched toward heaven, symbolized by Qian

For Qi to circulate, the body must also be rooted in the earth, symbolized by Kun

KUN

waning of the seasons, and was also used to predict the fortune of an individual from the young spring of life to the winter of old age.

For a practitioner of the fighting art of Baguazhang, combining the Eight Palm Changes with the Eight Triagrams also creates sixty-four possible combinations. The Circular Walking Baguazhang practitioner observes the opponent and, by assessing their disposition, can then initiate the correct response. This is based on the appropriate checks and balances of Yin and Yang and the relevant triagrams.

For example, the triagram Qian symbolizes heaven and the triagram Kun symbolizes earth. Within Baguazhang, Qian refers to the upright spine stretched toward heaven, which we rotate around as if the arms were the spokes of an umbrella. Kun refers to the principle of being rooted into the earth, so that we remain steady even when moving. Both these triagrams relate to Qi circulating around the body along The Small Circulation of Qi, up the back to the top of the head. corresponding to the triagram Qian (heaven), and then down the front of the body into the belly, corresponding to the triagram Kun (earth).

If Qi circulation is continuous and smooth, good health will be attained, martial power will be strong, and with balanced Qi, it will be easier to avoid emotional extremes and keep a calm mind,

THE EIGHT TRIAGRAM ANIMAL PALMS

The great Baguazhang Master, Sun Luc tang, explains in his book, *The Study of Bagua Fist* (1916), how each of the Eight Palm techniques of Baguazhang are associated not only with a triagram, but also with the qualities of certain animals, namely, the lion, the unicorn, the snake, the hawk, the dragon, the bear, the phoenix, and the monkey.

The Eight Triagrams are each associated with the characteristics of an animal.

Qian - Lion

In The Yi jing, the triagram Qian is symbolic of heaven. It is associated with the Lion, which is brave and violent by nature and can defeat most other creatures, and is expressed by the Baguazhang palm techniques known as Golden Dragon Opens its Mouth and White Ape Draws its Saber.

When practicing the Qian triagram palm, the movements should be explosive Fa jin strikes, vigorous and robust like a lion shaking its fur. The three straight lines of this triagram are like the lion's teeth and claws, and this makes our fighting spirit powerful and fierce. When the fingers are extended forcefully, in the manner of a lion extending its claws, the flow of Qi to the hands will be increased, and the fighting spirit will be formidable. Qian is also associated with Qi, which nourishes everything. It has unlimited variations just like the infinite applications of the Lion Palm.

The Qian triagram is also linked with the heart and the blood vessels, and when practiced smoothly and correctly, it will have a beneficial effect on the circulation.

The Qian triagram palm has features characteristic of the fighting spirit of its associated animal, the lion.

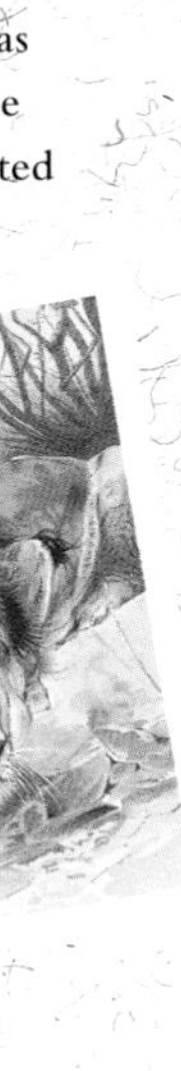

The fingers extend forward like the claws of a lion

Movements are fast and light

Kun - Unicorn

In The Yi jing the triagram Kun symbolizes Earth. This triagram is related to the Unicorn, a gentle-natured animal, and the Returning Body Palm Change. Kun is the most Yin triagram, so the palm change is characterized by yielding. The movements that best express the sybolism of the Kun triagram are Spreading Wings and White Crane Stands on one Leg.

It must be remembered that yielding does not refer to weakness or continuous defensive maneuvers. Rather it means that, like the Unicorn, movements can fly unpredictably where the opponent least expects. Yielding does not mean retreating - it means attacking again and again, from unexpected and obscure positions.

The body, when moving like the unicorn, can turn like a tornado and move with light, free, fast movements. This particular type of turning strengthens the Qi in the Lower Dan Dien, which will not only make the lower abdomen stronger but will also strengthen the spirit.

The Returning Body Palm Change is yielding, or unpredictable movements, characterized by the gentle unicorn.

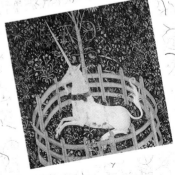

Kan - Snake

The triagram Kan in Baguazhang is an explanation of how to hold the correct body posture: relaxed on the outside but holding the correct firm structure. This is represented by the soft, broken Yin lines on the outside, and the hard, unbroken Yang lines on the inside.

Kan is associated with the Snake and is expressed by the Smooth Posture Palm. The Snake is sly, winding, and cunning, and this is clearly expressed by the twisting, turning, and continuously moving techniques of the Baguazhang fighter. When the snake moves one part of its sinuous anatomy, its whole body moves. The Snake spits venom suddenly, like the unpredictable Fa jin attacks from the Baguazhang practitioner.

In The Yi jing the triagram Kan is symbolic of Water. The way of applying the Smooth Posture Palm is to move like water, flowing smoothly with the ability to slip through any opening in the opponent's defense, just like water seeping through a crack. If the movements are fluid on the outside, Qi will be encouraged to flow on the inside.

In Traditional Chinese Medicine, Water balances Fire. So by nourishing the Water triagram Kan, our internal fire will be prevented from flaring up, and causing dizziness, headaches, and insomnia. When Fire and Water are balanced, it is easier to maintain a balance mentally and emotionally, and it is possible to develop a calm and clear spirit.

Movements are fluid

The movements of the Smooth Posture Palm are fluid, like the continuous movement of the snake.

Li - Hawk

The triagram Li is the Hawk. This bird of prey has its Periphery Vision attuned to such a degree that it picks up the movement of its prey subconsciously. It then continues to monitor and track its victim. When it is within range, the hawk locks onto the target and enters into a power dive. Then, with claws extended and flexed, it will impact with its prey. The hawk aims for specific points on its victim's body, but often just the shock of the impact itself is enough to stun its prey. This natural way of hunting, adopted by the Baguazhang fighter, will bring him victory every time.

The triagram Li is expressed in the posture known as the Lying Palm which should be practiced with firm movement on the outside - represented by the two outer Yang lines - and a mind that is free and able to adapt to changing circumstances - represented by the single Yin line inside. The Baguazhang practitioner should aim to be agile and versatile like the hawk flying at great speed through the forest, dodging and weaving its way between the branches.

In The Yi jing the triagram Li is associated with the element Fire. When practicing and applying Baguazhang, it is necessary to be fired up, a psychological state that can be encouraged by certain physical movements. When we are "fired up," all our Qi has been activated and made available for us to use. It goes to the body's surface and strengthens us against attack.

Qi is also sent to the hands and feet, or whatever parts of the body we are using to attack the opponent. If we are using a fist, when full of Qi it becomes like a hammer. If we are stabbing with our finger tips, when full of Qi they become like daggers. A further benefit of being fired up is that after training there is still a lot of Qi vigorously circulating around the body. This Qi can be used by the mind in a creative project, such writing or painting, or in any kind of endeavor.

Agility is characteristic of hawklike movement

Fighting like a hawk with a swift accurate attack is characteristic of the Lying Palm.

The smooth movements of the Dragon are portrayed through the Horizontal Lifting Palm.

The practitioner coils and uncoils in smooth movements

Zhen - Dragon

The triagram Zhen is expressed in the Horizontal Lifting Palm and is associated with the Dragon. In Chinese mythology and culture, the dragon is a spiritual being. It is immortal and can fly through the air. These are the spiritual qualities that the Baguazhang practitioner strives to develop. The smooth, powerful way a dragon moves is also expressed in the posture called Black Dragon Wrapping Around the Post. Baguazhang practitioners should aim to make their movements as smooth as a dragon coiling and uncoiling, as then the Qi and blood of the liver will flow smoothly around the body. If this is achieved, our vision will be good, our tendons strong and flexible, and our temperament will be moderate.

In The Yi jing the triagram Zhen is associated with Thunder. Baguazhang practitioners should make their Fa jin movements explosive just like Thunder.

Gen - Bear

The triagram Gen is expressed through the Baguazhang technique of the Back Body Palm and is associated with the Bear. One of the characteristics of the bear is the way it shakes its fur, and Baguazhang practitioners aim to shake their bodies in this way when they are applying their rotating twisting Fa jin. The bear also has great power in its back and limbs, and can lift and uproot trees. If the Back Body Palm is practiced correctly, the upper body will be strengthened, and the practitioner will be able to lift and uproot the opponent.

In The Yi jing the triagram Gen is associated with the Mountain and, when a Baguazhang practitioner has developed his Rooting ability, he or she becomes as stable as a mountain. At a more advanced level, it is possible to have the same degree of stability while moving as it is standing in one place.

The Back Body Palm strengthens the upper body so that, bearlike, the practitioner can uproot his opponent.

The practitioner is firmly rooted

Xun - Phoenix

The triagram Xun is expressed through the Baguazhang technique of the Wind Wheel Palm and is associated with the Phoenix. When the phoenix beats its wings, there are two aspects that relate to Baguazhang practice. First, if this motion is duplicated by the arms, a great breaking power is generated, both on the upward and on the downward movement. Second, if the hands move like feathers, this means that they trail behind the arm in the same way that a feather would were it to be held in the hand and moved gently from side to side.

Those who can make their external movements as smooth and all-embracing as the swirling wind are encouraging Qi to flow to every part of the body. For the fighting applications of Baguazhang, movements should be like a whirlwind. The opponent is drawn into a vortex of incredible power and then thrown out with great force. The spiraling power of a Baguazhang practitioner is like a hurricane smashing everything in its path, but retaining a calm center, the "eye of the storm."

The beating movements of the Wind Wheel Palm reflect the wing movements of the phoenix.

Hands trail behind like feathers in the wind

Dui - Monkey

The triagram Dui is expressed through the Baguazhang technique of the Embracing Palm and is associated with the Monkey. There are many aspects of the Monkey that can make a good Baguazhang practitioner a great Baguazhang fighter, if they are correctly understood and applied.

Although monkeys are the closest to humans on the evolutionary tree, the essential difference is that monkeys still retain their wildness. It is when we embrace this wildness that we become great fighters. Just as monkeys do not think about what techniques to use when they fight, so the Baguzhang fighter has to incorporate this wildness into what he is doing to make his self-defense work as a real survival art.

The Baguazhang practitioner should retain an element of wildness in his practice, representative of the untamed monkey.

The Embracing Palm is associated with the Monkey

THE FIGHTING APPLICATIONS OF BAGUAZHANG

The practitioner of Baguazhang has an almost unlimited number of possible fighting applications at his or her disposal. First, there are the combinations of the eight basic palm shapes that can be different in the lead hand and the rear hand. This eight-times-eight combination already gives us one variation of the sixty-four hexagrams of The Yi jing (see page 66). There are also the eight sets of movements called Palm Changes, which can be done in both a clockwise and counterclockwise direction, which give us another combination of the sixty-four hexagrams.

The linear form in Baguazhang is the Eight Palm Changes taken from the Circle Walking Form and changed slightly so that they are more orientated toward the martial applications. This is why this form is sometimes called the Baguazhang Fighting Form.

In the Circle Walking Form the Baguazhang practitioner looks through the Dragon's Mouth – this is the space between the thumb and index finger of the lead hand, which is almost always pointing toward the center of the circle, and is where the imagined opponent is.

It is not just the footwork of Baguazhang forms that is circular – so are its fighting applications. Deep, firm stepping around the opponent is used to sweep, trip, bodycheck, and throw him. The stepping in Baguazhang is called Muddy Walking. This has many meanings: first, the feet slide along as if the ground is muddy; second, because Rooting is so deep, it feels that the feet have become entrenched in muddy ground.

Also, by circling in closely, a Baguazhang practitioner can not only strike and grapple, but has the ability to also bodycheck the opponent with a rapid spinning movement.

In both attack and defense the extension and retraction of the palms is circular, often like a snake coiling around someone's arm.

When entering onto the opponent, the practitioner can choose the appropriate direction, either clockwise (Yang) or counterclockwise (Yin). The best approach is to enter on the outside of his lead hand so that he is less able to use his rear hand. This will also give access to many vulnerable areas on the exposed, unprotected side and the back.

Every movement in Baguazhang is circular like this, with Yin and Yang shifting and changing into one another. Weight goes from left to right leg, and back again. The body turns clockwise (Yang) and counterclockwise (Yin). The palms spiral out (Yang) and back (Yin) in a corkscrew motion. The palm strikes that result from the coiling and recoiling action of the twisting waist have great power, and the practitioner usually keeps one palm pointing toward the center while walking the Baguazhang circle. All these different movements that mobilize Qi are different manifestations of Yin and Yang.

For a practitioner of the fighting art of Baguazhang, combining the Eight Palm Changes with the Eight Triagrams creates sixty-four possible combinations. The circular walking Baguazhang practitioner observes the opponent, and by assessing their disposition can initiate the correct response based on the appropriate checks and balances of Yin and Yang and the relevant triagrams.

For example, if the opponent's right leg (Yang) is forward, but their weight is on the rear leg (Yin), they would appear to be in a defensive (Yin) posture, almost inviting an attack. However, there is no weight on the front leg, they are free to kick. The practitioner would then have to defend (Yin) against this first before using a counterattack (Yang within Yin).

It could be said that an attacking move is an expression of Yang Qi and a defensive move is an expression of Yin Qi. In reality, all movements are partly defensive and partly offensive, and contain a mixed combination of Yin and Yang Qi, just like the triagrams.

The moves themselves also correspond to the Yin and Yang qualities of the triagrams. For example, the triagram Qian is composed of three Yang lines, and a corresponding move has great force and

A Baguazhang Application

The Baguazhang response to the opponent's attack is to counterattack forward immediately with a series of Fa jin movements. These movements can be practiced against an imaginary opponent or slowly as a moving meditation sequence to get an idea of what this style feels like.

1. The opponent steps forward with the left foot and punches to the face of the Baguazhang practitioner with the left fist.

2. The Baguazhang practitioner responds using her right Mountain Palm to attack forward into the outside of the opponnent's left arm, (waist turns to the left) just above the elbow. At the same time she steps forward with her right foot to the outside of the opponent.

3. The Baguazhang practitioner thrusts her left Heaven Palm forward into the opponent's eyes (waist turns to the right).

power. A move that expresses the triagram Kun, which is made up of three Yin lines, would have a more defensive, evasive quality.

In Baguazhang we begin knowing nothing. Then, after many years of training, all the variations of the sixty-four hexagrams are literally in the palms of our hands. After attaining this high level of complexity, it is then time to return to simplicity, not just back to the Eight Triagrams, nor just back to their source, Yin and Yang, but right back to the point of origin of all of life's complexities. This means going back to the very source of life itself which is beyond opposites, the all-encompassing unity of spirit.

4. Her left hand grabs and pulls the opponent's left arm toward her as she folds her right arm in and, with her right elbow, she hits the opponent in his left temple (waist turns to the left).

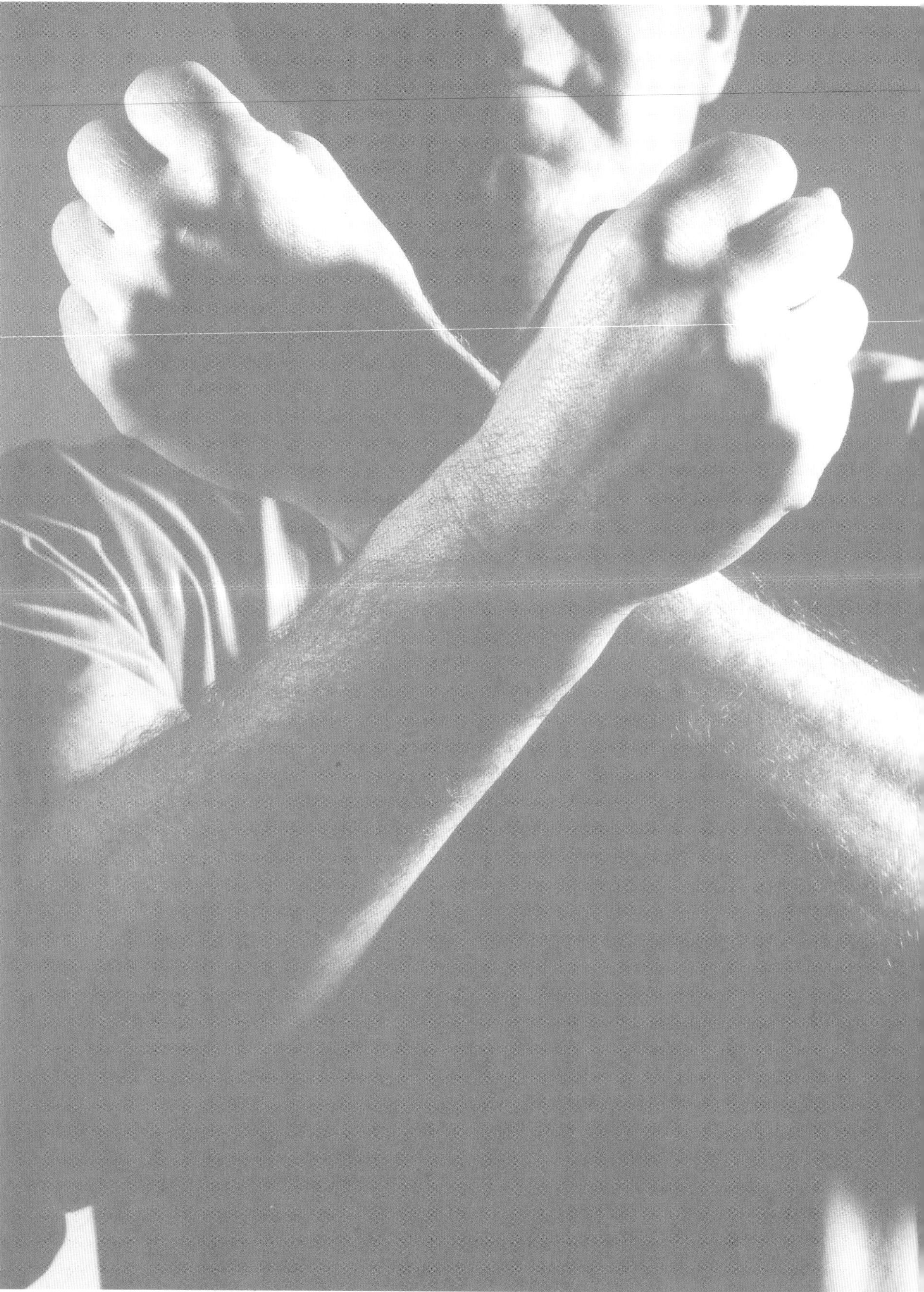

Xingyiquan

FORM INTENTION FIST

形意拳

ALTHOUGH XINGYIQUAN translates literally as "Form Intention Fist," the meaning is actually rather more complicated. The use of the word "fist" here means "martial art," and the word "form" refers to the variety of postures that are used in this style. "Intention" means the mind, and, in this case, the part of the mind that initiates action. Altogether Xingyiquan, or Form Intention Fist, describes a martial art that emphasizes body movement as a direct result of mental intention.

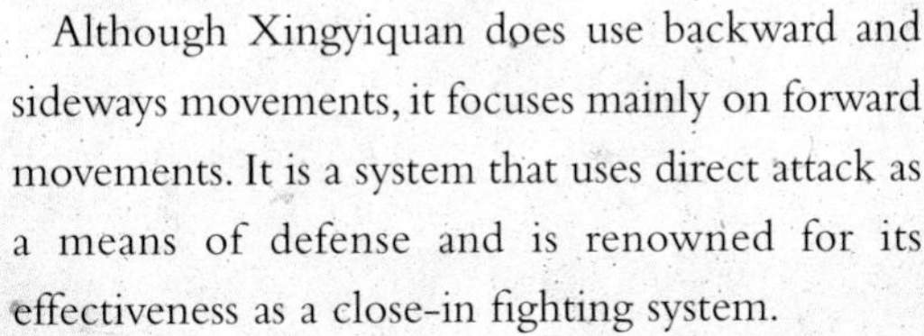

Although Xingyiquan does use backward and sideways movements, it focuses mainly on forward movements. It is a system that uses direct attack as a means of defense and is renowned for its effectiveness as a close-in fighting system.

The Xingyiquan system contains many different aspects. The best-known aspects are the Five Element forms of Wood, Fire, Earth, Metal, and Water, which in turn express the techniques of Pi, Tzuann, Beng, Pau, and Hern. There is also a linking sequence that is used to combine these different movements.

Xingyiquan is also famous for the Twelve Animal Fists that are expressed in the Twelve Animals Forms. There are a few different versions of the Twelve Animals of Xingyiquan, and not all practitioners use the same names or the same animals. The most common are Swallow, Hawk (sometimes called Sparrow), Monkey, Chicken (sometimes called Cock), Snake, Water Lizard (sometimes called Tortoise or Alligator), Eagle, Bear, Tiger, Horse, Phoenix (or Ostrich), and Dragon.

Xingyiquan also has a two-man fighting form that can be used to practice the applications of techniques learned in the other forms.

Xingyiquan – Form Intention Fist – uses direct attack controlled by the mind.

COMPARING XINGYIQUAN TO TAIJIQUAN AND BAGUAZHANG

Taijiquan is regarded as the mother of all the internal martial arts, Baguazhang the daughter, and Xingyiquan, the third most well-known, is known as the son. The emphasis in Xingyiquan is on attacking straight into the opponent, and the direct forward movements of its forms reflect this. Baguazhang, on the other hand, specializes in attacks from the side and is characterized by forms that are spiraling and twisting, with the aim of getting around the side of the opponent. Taijiquan forms have both circular and straight movements and, for self-defense, it makes use of both direct attacks and side attacks, depending on the circumstances. To the untrained observer, all three styles appear to be slightly

To the untrained eye, many of the internal martial arts look different. Their principles, however, are the same.

Xingyiquan movements are more linear, Baguazhang movements are more circular, while Taijiquan has both linear and circular movements.

Baguazhang concentrates on twisting, circular attacks from obscure angles

different. To the experienced martial artist, however, there are clearly many similarities between them, particularly internally, where the same principles apply. In their expression of power, Taijiquan is the softest, and its movements can be likened to a bullwhip. Baguazhang is slightly more firm its movements, like a spring coiling and uncoiling. Xingyiquan is the hardest and can be likened to a rattan cane.

All three styles share the principle of Fa jin point strikes; however, when it is applied with Taijiquan, there is no muscle tension in the hand on impact, and both fists and palm strikes are used. With Baguazhang the flex in the pounding palm is greater than in Taijiquan, and most of the time only the palms are used, not the fists. In Xingyiquan the fists are used much more, and on impact the striking fist has more tension.

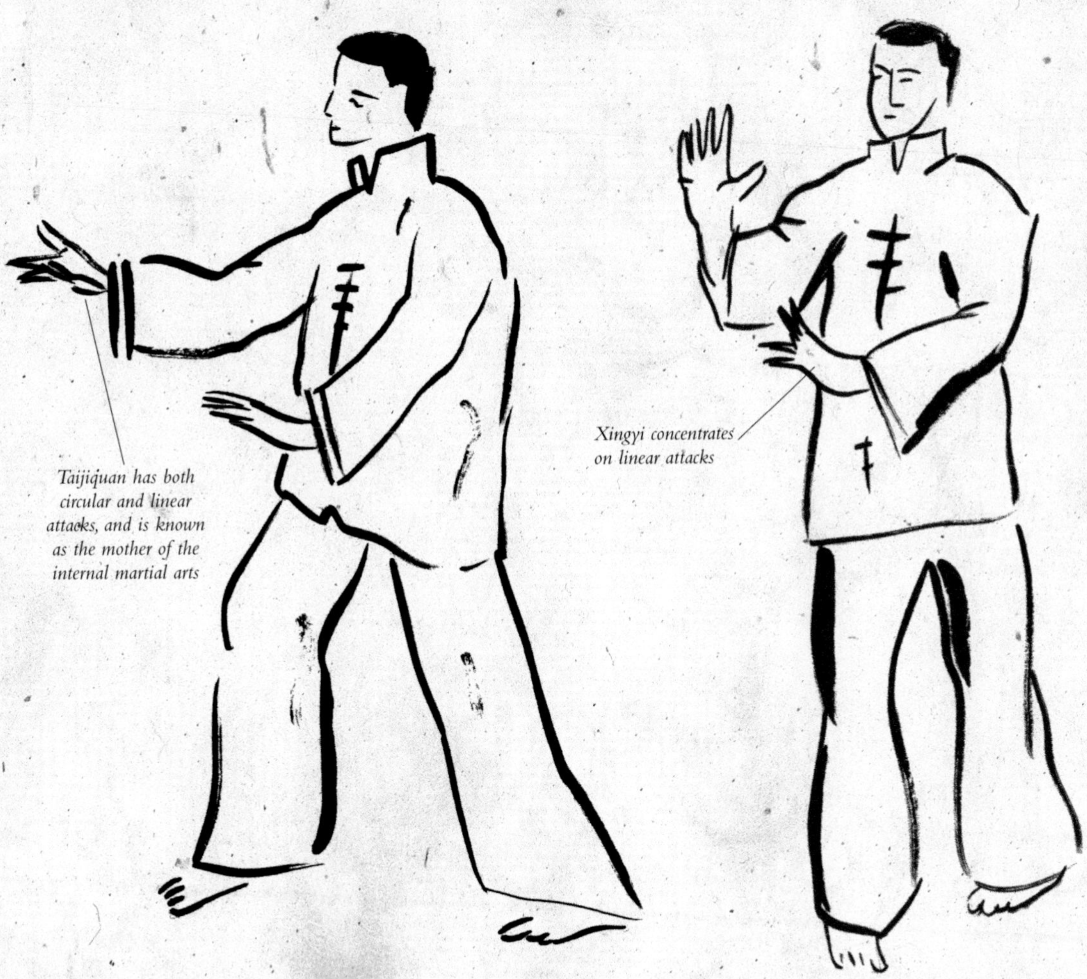

Taijiquan has both circular and linear attacks, and is known as the mother of the internal martial arts

Xingyi concentrates on linear attacks

HISTORY OF XINGYIQUAN

It is generally accepted that Xingyiquan had already been in existence for several centuries before General Yeuh Fei organized it into the system we have today. Indeed, there is much documentary evidence that the use of movements based on the characteristics of animals had been used in China for thousands of years. Such movements were sometimes used as Qigong health exercises and also for martial arts training.

General Yeuh Fei (born A.D.1103) was responsible for organizing Xingyiquan into the system we know today. By looking at his life we can gain an insight not just into the man who formulated Xingyiquan, but also into an exemplary traditional martial artist, to whom people still look as a model of the moral principles that should be cultivated in internal martial arts training: courage, integrity, and honor.

Some forms of Xingyiquan are named after animals and birds, one of which is the hawk.

The Life of General Yeuh Fei

Yeuh Fei was born into a time of great turmoil in China. War was raging on the northern border, the government was steeped in corruption, and fear of famine gripped the land. His father named him Yeuh Fei because it means "to fly," and he hoped that, in this time of unrest, Yeuh Fei would be able to rise above the disorder and achieve great things.

Although born into a poor family, Yeuh Fei learned to read and write and studied hard. He was particularly fascinated by a book called *The Art of War,* a collection of writings from the Warring States Period (476–221 B.C.). These writings had a profound effect on him, both in his military career and in his development in the martial arts. Indeed, the style in which General Yeuh Fei's theses on Xingyiquan are written is very similar to that of *The Art of War.*

He was an intelligent young man, and this potential was spotted early by a Shaolin monk who lived locally. The monk decided to take him on as his student, and Yeuh Fei learned everything that the monk knew. Some people say that it was from this monk that Yeuh Fei learned Xingyiquan and that the true origins of the art are in fact in the Shaolin Monastery. Other people say that like Taijiquan, Xingyiquan comes from Wudang Mountain. As with all martial arts, its origins and true history remain vague.

At the age of 20, Yeuh Fei joined the army of the Southern Song Dynasty, struggling to regain land lost to the northern invaders, a nomadic tribe called the Gin. Yeuh Fei excelled as a soldier. His martial arts skills made him a great fighter, and his study of *The Art of War* made him a fine strategist. His talents and skills were rewarded with promotion time after time, and in only six years he had reached the exalted rank of General. General Yeuh Fei was then given command of the army that was fighting the northern Gin. He immediately began to apply his knowledge of individual combat and war strategy to the army. The soldiers were taught Xingyiquan, and the army was reorganized to become an efficient fighting force. His personal charisma and effective strategies in both organizing and running an army made people gather to his banner. He was a wise and honorable man who was determined to create a fighting force that would defeat the northern Gin and reclaim the land that the Chinese Southern Song Dynasty had lost to them.

General Yeuh Fei was a great war strategist, credited with using and organizing Xingyiquan into the forms we know today.

General Yeuh Fei was not only an expert at the martial art of Xingyiquan, he was also very knowledgeable in the practice of Qigong and is credited with the creation of the Qigong set of movements called The Eight Piece Brocade.

Victory after victory against the Gin followed as Yeuh Fei advanced north with his army. It was thus in the forge of battle that Xingyiquan was tried, tested, and refined. General Yeuh Fei defeated all the forces sent against him by the Gin and was a shining example to his troops of what a martial artist should be: wise, courageous, and honorable. People who train Xingyiquan (or any of the internal martial arts) today should not only try to increase their Qi, strengthen their spirit, and improve their health, but also develop these good qualities within themselves. General Yueh Fei succeeded honorably in battle, but was finally defeated by treachery.

He was brought down by the politician Chin Kua, who held a high position in the court of the Emperor. Chin Kua accepted a bribe from the leaders of the Gin to destroy General Yeuh Fei. Unknown to the Emperor, Chin Kua issued a royal summons to the General, insisting that he come to the court of the Emperor immediately. General Yeuh Fei could not understand why, when his military campaign in the north was going so well, he should be recalled to the south. However, he could not refuse a royal command and so returned to the capital. Upon his arrival the evil Chin Kua had him imprisoned and then murdered in A.D. 1142. He was defeated by a man who displayed all the characteristics that practitioners of the internal martial arts try to rid themselves of: namely, greed, jealousy, lying, and egotistic self-advancement.

At the age of just 39, General Yueh Fei, a man who had achieved so much, was dead. His honor, courage, and integrity live on in the art of Xingyiquan, and his story is an example to all martial artists. We are fortunate that he wrote down his understanding of the art of Xingyiquan in his famous book, *Yeuh Fei's Ten Important Theses*. It is from this work that almost all other writings on Xingyiquan are derived.

THE FIVE ELEMENTS FORMS OF XINGYIQUAN

Xingyiquan is based on the theory of the Five Elements and their various interactions. This theory of the Five elements is a major aspect of Traditional Chinese Medicine. It shows the relationship between all the different parts of the body and the way in which the body is affected by the environment.

In Xingyiquan the Five Elements forms are said to strengthen the corresponding internal organs by increasing their Qi. The Wood form Beng strengthens the Liver, the Fire form Pau strengthens the Heart, the Earth form Heng strengthens the Spleen, the Metal form Pi strengthens the Lungs, and the Water form Tzuann strengthens the Kidneys.

If the Liver is healthy, the tendons will be strong and the eyesight good. If the Heart is healthy, the blood vessels will be strong and the circulation vigorous. If the Spleen is adequately nourished, the muscles will be strong and the appetite good. If the Lungs are healthy, the skin will be firm and look good, and the sense of smell sharp. If the Kidneys are healthy, the bones will be strong and the hearing good.

Five Element theory is used in Traditional Chinese Medicine to show the relationship between the different parts of the body and the environment in which we live.

ELEMENT	Wood	Fire	Earth	Metal	Water
ORGAN	Liver	Heart	Spleen	Lungs	Kidneys
YANG EMOTION	Anger	Hate and Impatience	Worry and Anxiety	Sadness and Depression	Fear
YIN EMOTION	Kindness	Love, Joy, and Respect	Fairness and Openness	Uprightness and Courage	Gentleness
EXPRESSION	Shouting	Laughing	Singing	Weeping	Groaning
SEASON	Spring	Summer	Late Summer	Autumn	Winter
WEATHER	Wind	Heat	Dampness	Dryness	Cold
COLOR	Green	Red	Yellow	White	Black
CYCLE	Growing	Fruitful	Ripe Harvest	Seed Falling	Sleeping
TIME	Infancy	Youth	Adult	Old Age	Death
SENSE	Eyes	Tongue	Lips and Mouth	Nose	Ears
TASTE	Sour	Bitter	Sweet	Pungent	Salty
NOURISHES	Nails, Tendons, and Nerves	Blood and Vessels	Muscles	Skin and Hair	Bones, Teeth, and Pubic Hair

Beng corresponds to the Wood element and strengthens the tendons.

Beng

The Beng form is executed with a powerful extending movement, like bamboo being bent back and then released, or a bow being drawn and the arrow released. Beng corresponds to the element Wood, and if its techniques are mastered, tendons will be resilient and pliable, and the liver will function smoothly. A branch of the Liver Meridian ascends up into the head, so the Beng form also nourishes the brain.

Pau

The Pau form uses techniques that are released like cannon fire from a gun. It is a powerful and explosive form and corresponds to the element Fire. If practiced correctly, Pau will strengthen the heart and maintain emotional balance by blasting out of the system any stagnant Qi or unexpressed emotions trapped in the heart.

Pau corresponds to the Fire element and strengthens the Heart.

Hern

The Hern form corresponds with the Spleen and its techniques are rounded and balanced. It is associated with the element Earth, and when we practice this movement, the center becomes stable and firm.

Hern corresponds to the Earth element and strengthens the Spleen.

Pi

The Pi form is an attacking form that is characterized by cleaving, rending, and splitting movements, like an ax cutting and chopping through wood. It corresponds to the element Metal and should be practiced with the correct breathing to strengthen the lungs.

Pi corresponds to the Metal element and strengthens the Lungs.

Tzuann

The Tzuann form corresponds to the element Water, and its movements are smooth and flowing. If practiced correctly, it will strengthen the kidneys. The fists twist upward with a drilling quality, while one hand pulls the opponent down.

Tzuann corresponds to the Water element and strengthens the Kidneys.

CREATIVE AND DESTRUCTIVE CYCLES OF THE FIVE TECHNIQUES

The outside arrows indicate the Creative Cycle of the Five Elements forms. Tzuann leads to the use of the movement Beng, in the same way that Water nourishes Wood (trees). Beng leads to the use of Pau, in the same way that Wood burns to make Fire. Pau leads to the use of Heng, in the same way that the ashes of Fire become Earth. Heng leads to the use of Pi in the same way that Metal is mined from Earth.

The inside arrows indicate the Destructive Cycle of the Five Elements Forms. Heng can be used to defeat the technique of Tzuann in the same way that the Earth banks of a river control Water. Tzuann can be used to defeat Pau in the same way that Water puts out Fire. Pau is effective against Pi in the same way that Fire will melt Metal. Pi will defeat Beng in the same way that a metal ax can smash Wood.

The Constructive Cycle (outside) and the Destructive Cycle (inside) show the relationship between the Five Elements.

THE TWELVE ANIMAL FORMS OF XINGYIQUAN

When practicing the Twelve Animal forms, it is not just a question of trying to imitate an animal, but of expressing its qualities. Each form has a different emphasis that helps cultivate a particular skill. This skill can then be put into all the other animal forms, as well as the Five Element forms.

The Swallow form develops muscle suppleness and a responsive mind.

The Hawk form (sometimes called the Sparrow) activates the Lower Dan Dien and strengthens the middle body.

The Swallow Form

The Hawk form

The Monkey form

The Monkey form calms the spirit, strengthens the mind, and develops an upright posture.

The Chicken form (sometimes called the Fighting Cock) strengthens the liver and Qi supply to the head. It also strengthens the legs, making them speedy and resilient. (The chicken may seem to be an unusual animal to pick for a martial art form; however, cockfighting is very popular in Asia, where the animals stab each other with their claws and smash each other with their wings - very different from the generally docile chickens that are found in the West!)

The Snake form develops continuous, flowing movements. The body should also move like a

THE SNAKE FORM

THE CHICKEN FORM

THE WATER LIZARD FORM

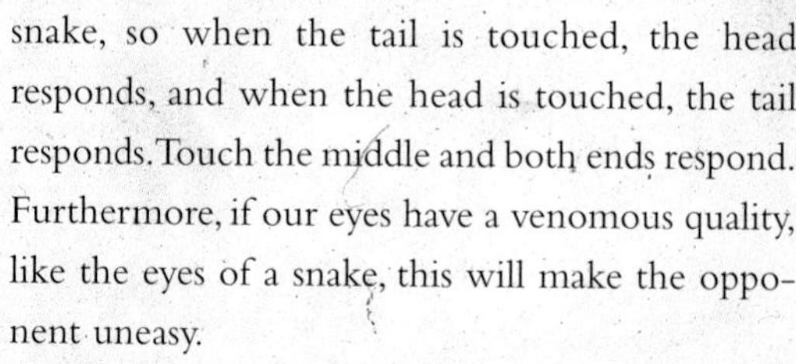

THE BEAR FORM

snake, so when the tail is touched, the head responds, and when the head is touched, the tail responds. Touch the middle and both ends respond. Furthermore, if our eyes have a venomous quality, like the eyes of a snake, this will make the opponent uneasy.

The Water Lizard form (sometimes called the Tortoise or the Alligator) strengthens the spleen and stomach and makes us more grounded.

The Bear form emphasizes the roundness of the bear's shoulders, and its calm and steady nature.

The Tiger form teaches us to roar as we attack and to be furious in our movements, like a tiger leaping on a lamb.

THE HORSE FORM

THE TIGER FORM

THE PHOENIX FORM

The Horse form strengthens the heart and clears away excessive anger.

The Phoenix form (sometimes called the Ostrich) strengthens the kidneys and balances the Small Circulation of Qi.

The Dragon form clears excess heat from the body, and gives us the alertness of a dragon. It allows the body to move in a curved, flowing dragonlike way.

The Eagle form is central to Xingyiquan because in every attack, whatever movement we are performing, the mind always has an attacking intention toward the opponent, like a fierce eagle impacting with its prey.

THE DRAGON FORM

THE EAGLE FORM

THE FA JIN OF XINGYIQUAN

In Xingyiquan Fa jin attacks are released with incredible force. Qi is mobilized from the Lower Dan Dien by the Fa jin to reach and nourish the five extremities: hair, tongue, teeth, skin, and nails. This may be so powerful that it makes the hair stand on end, in the same way that a cat's hair stands on end when it is threatened.

Fa jin also hints at the development of a sixth sense, hence the expression "I could tell someone was looking at me because the hairs on the back of my head stood up."

Because the blood follows the movement of Qi, the skin goes red as the Qi rises up from the Lower Dan Dien to the surface of the body. This invigoration of the system is not only beneficial for health, but is also very helpful in a self-defense situation.

The Qi buildup on the surface of the body gives greater protection against the attacker's blows as we counterattack.

The Xingyiquan Fa jin is always a forward attacking movement. The practitioner leaps forward, and the energy generated from the foot stamping on the ground flows up through the body and is released through the attacking fist.

The tongue reflects the state of the muscles in the body, and when Qi rises up, the tongue rises up to connect to the top of the mouth. This allows the Qi to circulate freely around the body along the Small Circulation of Qi. In a Fa jin attack, Qi rushes into the muscles, thereby giving them greater power and the ability to achieve remarkable feats of strength.

The teeth are the ends of the bones and, in Xingyiquan, the teeth are kept clenched together so that the face is set with a determined expression.

The nails are the ends of the tendons, and the tendons are like the string of an archer's bow. They are used to release the Fa jin power throughout the body, all the way to the ends of the fingers, toes, and the nails.

The idea of the Fa jin beginning in the Lower Dan Dien and then moving out to the five extremities of the body is compared in Xingyiquan to the imagery of a tree: when the trunk of the tree (the torso) shakes, the branches and leaves (hands and feet) shake as well.

THE EXTERNAL ALIGNMENT FOR XINGYIQUAN

In Xingyiquan the structural alignment of the body is very important for improving health, increasing the flow of Qi, and, in self-defense, for the correct transference of power throughout the whole body.

Many parts of the body need to be synchronized and move together in pairs. For example, the nose must be kept over the navel to make sure that the head and body move together. The shoulders must move in accordance with the hip bones: this will unify the upper and lower body movement. The elbows and the knees must move together as a pair, as must the hands and feet. Finally, the hands must be kept on the center line of the body that runs from the nose to the navel.

In the self-defense applications of Xingyiquan, the head, shoulders, elbows, hands, hips, knees, and feet are all coordinated together so that when one part of the body is used to hit the opponent, it is supported by the weight and momentum of the whole body. All these parts of the body can be used as weapons to strike the opponent.

Usually one hand is held up and the other down. This is so that one can block high attacks and counterstrike low, or vice versa. Also, one can feign a high attack causing the opponent's guard to move up, thus opening them to a low attack.

If the body parts are all synchronized, then our movements, whether they are slow, fast, or as a Fa jin explosive movement, will be balanced and coordinated. Qi will then flow smoothly without hindrance.

Elbows should also be kept relatively low and close to the body most of the time. This is so that the ribs can be protected, and because the attacks in Xingyiquan are direct frontal strikes, the hands can extend out in front to strike directly. Almost all Xingyiquan techniques can be likened to a boxer's jab punch, rather than a hook punch, and its applications are almost all related to the direct frontal attack.

Correct alignment of the body is a vital part of Xingyiquan.

THE INTERNAL ALIGNMENT FOR XINGYIQUAN

In Xingyiquan it is important that all the various internal aspects of the body are integrated. First, breathing must be coordinated with body movement, so when we strike there is a simultaneous exhalation and abdominal movement. The breathing techniques of the internal martial arts are centered around the abdomen area, rather than the chest (see page 24). The chest is usually kept relaxed, and it is the abdomen that is expanded and contracted by the inhalation and exhalation of the breath. The Lower Dan Dien energy center is also activated by this type of breathing, and Qi can be pumped from there to all other parts of the body.

Inhalation and exhalation, and accompanying abdominal movement, is done in coordination with the extension and retraction of the arms and legs. This powerful pumping action increases Qi creation, invigorates its circulation, and results in martial applications having greater force.

Second, the forward Fa jin must be balanced by the correct use of Rooting. If the posture is not rooted, then there will be no foundation for power.

Finally, the balancing of the emotional mind and the wisdom mind is the hardest of all the pairs to coordinate. The wisdom mind is in the head and makes logical, clear-thinking decisions. The emotional mind is in the heart and is concerned more with feelings than with thoughts. In a conflict both the emotional mind and the wisdom mind

---

A Xingyiquan Application

The Xingyiquan response to the opponent's attack is to counterattack forward immediately with a series of Fa jin movements.

These movements can be practiced against an imaginary opponent or as a little moving meditation sequence to obtain an idea of what this style feels like.

1. *The opponent steps forward with the left foot, punching the solar plexus of the Xingyiquan practitioner with her left fist.*

are activated: we usually have an emotional response to a situation, and use our clear thinking mind to channel the emotional energy created by our heart mind into our counterattack so it will have more power.

We should allow fear (adrenalin) and anger generated by the emotional mind to grow and channel this Qi into an explosive Fa jin movement to give it more force. Fa jin movements are usually accompanied with a shout. This is a combination of breath being released into the movement, along with the Qi of our fear and anger. The energy is led by our intention, through the body into the strike at the opponent.

Ultimately in a conflict, whether verbal or physical, we need both the wisdom mind and the

2. The Xingyiquan practitioner responds by stepping forward with his right foot, and uses his right Wood Fist to attack forward into the inside of the opponent's left arm (this deflects the opponent's punch away to the outside). He then extends this further to punch the opponent in the left floating rib.

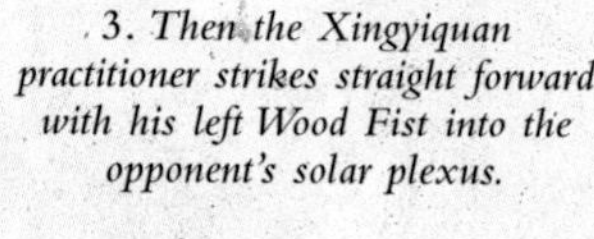

3. Then the Xingyiquan practitioner strikes straight forward with his left Wood Fist into the opponent's solar plexus.

emotional mind to work together in a balanced way. If the emotional mind dominates, anyone can "push our buttons" and send us off on an emotional rollercoaster. If our wisdom mind is in control, though we have the benefit of clear thought, we are cold and unfeeling toward others.

We need to understand all the complexities of our wisdom mind, just as we need to understand the varied emotions that we feel in our heart from our emotional mind.

The internal balancing of the two minds is essential, because our thoughts and feelings affect Qi: if they are in disarray, then our Qi will be scattered and we will have no power for our martial art, no strength to maintain our health, and no foundation to develop our spirit.

4. *The practitioner then grabs and pulls down the opponent's right arm with his left hand while he re-attacks with his right fist.*

合氣道

Aikido

WAY OF SPIRITUAL HARMONY

AIKIDO IS AN INTERNAL martial art from Japan. Aiki means "the bringing together of Ki energy" and do means "the way." Aikido then translates as "The Way of Spiritual Harmony."

Although Aikido is from Japan, not China, many of the principles are the same as in the Chinese internal martial arts. The life force energy known in Chinese as Qi, is called Ki by the Japanese, while the Chinese Lower Dan Dien the Japanese call the Hara. Atemi is the Japanese name for Fa jin point strikes.

Aikido was developed and practiced in nineteenth-century Japan.

Aikido was created by Morihei Uyeshiba, who was recognized during his own lifetime as being a bright, shining light in the world of Japanese martial arts. He took various elements from Japan's different styles and forged them in the cauldron of his own personal experience to create Aikido.

To understand the art of Aikido, it is necessary to look at the life of the art's founder, Morihei Uyeshiba. His journey of self-discovery, through adventure and relentless training, allowed him to find his own truth, and he left behind him the legacy of an internal martial arts system that others could also use to find their own way.

Throughout his life his techniques changed: when he was young his movements were hard and physical. Then, in middle age, his skill became more an expression of internal power and his techniques became more flowing. This was possible because he was transcending the physical world, and allowing universal energy Ki to flow through him. Even in old age, his ability remained unequaled. By this time he was working with spiritual forces, and as a result none could touch him.

The reason that there are so many different variations in Aikido today is because of the various stages of Morihei's development. Morihei would teach his students what he was practicing at that time. He was constantly changing and developing his techniques, making them more spiritual and less physical.

Some people today want to have the same spiritual power as Morihei had, but do not realize they have to build a strong foundation first. Indeed, Morihei's development took decades. He began as an external martial artist using physical, hard, and forceful training, and eventually he developed into an internal martial artist using Ki energy and soft, flowing, spiritual movements.

THE LIFE OF MORIHEI UYESHIBA

Morihei Uyeshiba was born in 1883 in Tanabe village, in the Wakayama Prefecture of Japan. He was born prematurely and as a child was weak and frail. He was encouraged to train in the martial arts, in particular the art of Sumo, by his father, who was descended from samurai, and his grandfather, who was a respected martial artist of great ability and power. He was made stronger from working in the local agricultural and fishing community: working the land built up his strength and standing in a rocking boat and harpooning fish developed his balance and accuracy.

During his youth he immersed himself in the traditions and beliefs of Shinto and the mystical and spiritual techniques and practices that were unique to that part of Japan. He believed in the spirits and their ability to protect him, and throughout his life, he claimed that his abilities came as a result of their guidance.

As a teenager he went to work in Tokyo and further increased his martial arts ability there by training in Ju-jutsu. In 1903 he was conscripted into the army, where he learned the art of bayonet fighting. The mental element of this form of combat was total commitment and decisiveness: in war there were no second chances. Later in life, after he had formulated Aikido, one of the things he noted about his art clearly reflects this early training. He claimed that one has to advance at the enemy moving forward and to the side to avoid his attack, and then without hesitation strike him down. This technique is one of the central elements of the self-defense applications of Aikido and is called Issoku Irimi, or One-Step Entering.

The Wakayama area of Japan where Morihei Uyeshiba spent his formative years.

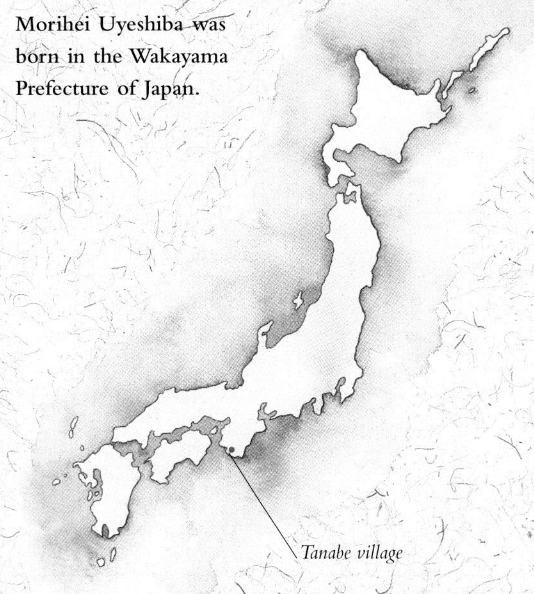

Morihei Uyeshiba was born in the Wakayama Prefecture of Japan.

In 1912 he led an expedition comprising over 50 families to set up a new community on the island of Hokkaido. It was during this period that Morihei developed incredible physical strength and endurance, routinely chopping down at least two trees every day, pulling the stumps clean out the ground, and chopping up the branches with his bare hands.

It was on Hokkaido that he met one of his most influential teachers, the fierce warrior Sokaku Takeda. Sokaku Takeda was a Master of the art of Daito Ryu Aikijutsu and, in his mid-forties, was approaching the peak of his power. Sokaku was also expert in the use of the spear and sword, and had killed many opponents in unarmed combat. He practiced Karate and also inherited the Oshiki Uchi fighting system from its only surviving practitioner, a priest called Saigo Tanomo. Sokaku was illiterate and did not care for much except for his martial arts. He taught Morihei much of his art on Hokkaido and continued to teach him intermittently over the years back in Japan.

During his time on Hokkaido, a spiritual balance to this fierce aspect was being cultivated within Morihei. He spent much of his time in the mountains attuning himself to the rhythms and cycles of nature. The flow of natural energy that he was starting to tap into would later become an integral principle of Aikido. He wrote about this phenomena many years later, saying that Aikido was not just a way of fighting, but was also a system that one could use to bring one's own Ki into harmony with the Ki of the Universe and ultimately become one with it.

Morihei Uyeshiba was a descendant from samurai and had a strong background in the martial arts.

Another influence on Morihei's spiritual development was his involvement in a new religious movement called Omotokyo. This was led by a charismatic figure called Onisaburo Deguchi, whose mission it was "to reform the world, heal the sick, and create heaven on earth." Morihei was very moved by this message and, in 1921, left the island of Hokkaido and went to study the meditation techniques taught at Ayabe on mainland Japan where Omotokyo had its main center of activities.

Morihei Uyeshiba was a great teacher of his martial art.

While he was there he learned about purification fasts, prayers, and rituals. With the encouragement of Onisaburo, Morihei started to teach martial arts to the other members of the group. There was a strong political revolutionary element to the Omotokyo movement and, sensing that his antagonistic and controversial speeches could be putting his life in danger, Onisaburo asked Morihei to be his personal bodyguard. Morihei's next big adventure was to accompany Onisaburo on a mission to China and Mongolia to spread the teachings of the cult Omotokyo.

It was here on the great rugged plains of Mongolia that Morihei put in place some of the most important pieces of the jigsaw puzzle that would eventually be Aikido.

On one occasion, Morihei defeated several huge Mongolian warriors by using explosive Atemi strikes (known as Fa jin point strikes in Chinese).

As a young man, Morihei studied the martial arts on the Japanese island of Hokkaido.

ABOVE As an old man, Morihei continued to demonstrate and teach Aikido, placing emphasis upon spiritual development.

LEFT It was while he was in the Mongolian plains that Morihei finally drew the strands of his experience together to form Aikido.

These successful strikes became key parts of Morihei's Aikido. (Today, however, this part of the system is taught only to advanced students.)

It was also during this time that Morihei was exposed to Chinese martial arts. It is thought that these influenced him, as there are many similarities between the Chinese internal martial art of Baguazhang and Aikido.

There was one moment during Morihei's Mongolian adventure when he came very close to death, but his developing spiritual powers saved him. The expedition was struck by a hail of bullets from a Chinese infantry patrol. Morihei remained calm and entered a meditative state. In his mind's eye lines of light revealed where the bullets were going and he was able to avoid them.

The Chinese army eventually caught up with the expedition, and they were immediately deported back to Japan. Onisaburo was thrown in jail, and Morihei went into retreat in the mountains of Kumano. Here he intensified his training and spent almost every available hour of every day practicing either martial arts or meditation. He was in his early forties, and the line between meditation and martial arts had vanished: every martial move he made was done in a state of meditation.

It was at this time that Morihei refined his ability to perceive lines of light that indicated the intention of the opponent's cuts and thrusts. He could now defeat any swordsman who challenged him, even if he was unarmed. Clearly he had reached a level of perception that only a few can hope to attain. By using the force of Ki rather than being reliant just on his physical strength, he reached an astoundingly high level of ability.

When Morihei started teaching Aikido, he tried to explained to his students what he had discovered, but not everyone could grasp what he meant. He would say that by maintaining the idea of peace not conflict in the mind, one would be in harmony with the universe. If we are attacked, the opponent's desire for conflict would be in opposition to universal harmony and so could not succeed. Aikido always wins because it is in tune with the universal Ki. Aggressiveness only leads to defeat.

The tales told of Morihei's apparently superhuman abilities are still talked of in Aikido training rooms today. Morihei could not only remain untouched by any attacker, whether armed or unarmed, but could also leap over their heads to avoid them.

Morihei moved to Tokyo in 1927 and because of his outstanding ability had many students who were devoted to him. However, following ancient tradition, he also had a number of people challenge him openly and also unexpectedly. He was always victorious, though, and became known within his own lifetime as one of Japan's greatest martial artists. In combat he could physically pick people up and throw them to the ground, or upset their balance when they attacked and cause them to appear as if they were throwing themselves.

There are stories about Morihei that suggest that he had transcended the laws of space and time, and could achieve things that were beyond the ability of any normal man. Morihei himself attributed his skills to spiritual forces, and insisted that only by embracing universal harmony and a love of all things would a person be able to reach the highest level.

He attracted a huge following from all over Japan and was invited to give a demonstration to the Emperor Hirohito. He was also invited to be personal instructor and bodyguard to the Imperial Family and to give instruction to high-ranking members of the police force, army, and navy.

1920s' Tokyo where Morihei taught Aikido, a skill he performed with great panache.

The advent of World War II led Morihei, a former warrior, to flee its destructiveness, which he now shunned as opposed to the principles of Aikido.

In 1942, at the outbreak of World War II, Morihei retired from the busy life he was leading in Tokyo and went to live in the countryside at a place called Iwama. Although he had been eager to further the interests of Japan when he was younger, he now did not want anything to do with the war. He saw the violence as being diametrically opposed to the principles of Aikido by which he lived his life. He believed that the purpose of Aikido was to cultivate respect, love, and peace and to align one's own Ki with the flow of universal Ki. Only in this way could one find peace within oneself.

At Iwama he returned to the land, farming and attuning himself with nature. Every day he prayed and meditated, and was only able to feel comfortable within himself when the war ended in 1945.

In his later years, his followers took care of running his Aikido schools and teaching classes. Although he occasionally taught and gave demonstrations, he concentrated mainly on developing further his own skill and spiritual insight. At the age of 60 he could still defeat heavyweight Sumo wrestlers who weighed almost three times as much as he did.

Morihei maintained the importance of training for combat effectiveness right into his old age, but also always stressed the value of Aikido for spiritual development.

Morihei Ueshiba, whose name means "Abundant Peace," died in 1969 at the age of 86 of liver cancer.

Morehei lived to be an old man, content to meditate and develop his own spiritual insight.

SCHOOLS OF AIKIDO

Today there are many different schools of Aikido, and they all teach in a different way. This is for a number of different reasons. Morihei himself was constantly changing his system as he developed. When he was young, his techniques were a result of his physical power; when he was middle-aged, they were accomplished by using Ki power; and in old age his ability was a manifestation of spiritual force. Depending on when a student was being taught by him, they would have received a different emphasis in their techniques, which would have been reflected when they began teaching themselves.

Also, some people have only been taught certain parts of the Aikido system, so when they teach themselves, their students believe they are receiving the complete system. For example, Aikido contains training with the sword, the staff, and uses direct counter attacks to vital points on the opponent's body known as Atemi. Many people are unaware of this and think that Aikido is just a system of throws and locking and controlling techniques.

The other school of Aikido concentrates on direct frontal strikes.

One school of Aikido concentrates on evasive, circular movements with locks and throws emphasized.

THE PRINCIPLES OF AIKIDO

Morihei was defeated only once in his life and that was by his teacher Sokaku who himself had developed a principle that became central to Aikido. Sokaku stressed the importance of unifying the body, breath, mind, and Ki in every movement, so that not only would the five senses develop, but also a further "sixth sense" could be cultivated. Morihei made this principle a central theme of all his Aikido movements.

Another important principle within Aikido is Kiai. This is a type of shout that combines special breathing techniques with the energy of Ki. It is used to psychologically unbalance the opponent as one counterattacks. At an advanced level, Kiai can cause serious damage to the opponent, and at the least it will unbalance them. Many people do not believe that this is possible; however, when we remember that the voice of a trained singer can shatter a glass, it is clear that the powerful vibrations that can be emitted by the human voice have great force. High-level practitioners are reputed to have a Kiai that can not be heard, but that is capable of knocking an opponent unconscious from a distance.

Morihei said that the way to penetrate to the heart of reality was by understanding Kiai. To do this, one has to know how to breath and to understand Ki. Then comes self-knowledge.

Aikido has its roots in the samurai traditions of Japan.

Morihei developed his system of Aikido over many years, constantly changing his approach.

Only by knowing oneself can one know others and only then will we find victory. Morihei stressed that through self-knowledge one could become aquainted with the underlying principles of Aikido: to purify the mind and body and connect with the spiritual world, in order to attain enlightenment.

Not many practitioners of Aikido today practice sword-fighting. However, an understanding of how to use and move with the sword is essential because many of the empty-hand movements are based on the techniques of sword-fighting. Furthermore, Morihei believed that, in the same way that the swordsman cuts down his opponent, so we should strive to rid ourselves of our own negative traits.

ENTERING

The use of weapons in Aikido is based on the principle of "entering." Entering means stepping in toward the opponent. Correct timing is essential for this to work properly. As the opponent is about to strike, by reaching out he or she creates an opening. The practitioner senses their aggressive intentions and, making use of the opening created by them, "enters."

Entering can vary from practitioner to practitioner. A person who trained with Morihei when he was older would have learned to use an Aikido throwing, locking, and controlling technique after entering. A person who trained with Morihei when he was younger would have learned to use Atemi explosive strikes to vital points after entering. Someone who had learned both techniques would be able to use whichever one was appropriate for the particular circumstances in which they found themselves.

Morihei's sensitivity to other people's Ki energy was so highly developed that he would know their intentions in advance. He was able to move just before they moved, and rush in and strike them down. He was in a state of tranquility, neither aggressive nor passive, neither defensive nor attacking. He was balanced and calm within himself, and in tune with the universe. The offensive intention of the opponent disrupted the harmony of the universe, and Morihei's response was a reflexive rebalancing of the disruption to the universal flow of Ki resonating within him.

Because of his highly developed sensitivity, Morihei knew in advance where the opponent was going to be. He could use the skillful footwork of his entering technique to end up standing next to them, looking where they were looking, at the spot in which he had just been standing. Then, because he was so finely balanced and so well positioned, he could use a throwing technique that was so well timed and executed that the opponent appeared to throw themselves.

The ability to be facing an attacker one moment, and then entering and standing next to them the next, can become so highly developed that it seems to the opponent that we disappear and reappear somewhere else. However, this ability takes decades to develop. Aikido can make us so balanced within, and so in tune with our and our opponent's Ki energy, that the normal laws of space and time seem to be transcended.

Some practitioners of Aikido use weapons with direct frontal attacks, entering or moving toward their opponent.

THE SPIRITUAL ASPECTS OF AIKIDO

The highest level of Aikido is only possible by embracing universal harmony and cultivating a love of all things. Only then can the true spiritual nature of existence be comprehended. Aikido teaches that in real life combat, there is no etiquette, no rules, and no fixed techniques. However, when training in Aikido, it is important to show respect for the divine spirit that animates all things and from which we receive our spiritual body. Also vital is a respect toward our parents, from whom we receive our physical body, and a respect for nature, which sustains us from day to day. Finally Aikido stresses the importance of showing respect for other people, hence in Aikido training rooms, there is a code of conduct that all students follow.

Throughout his whole life Morihei held deep beliefs about the underlying spiritual nature of reality. He prayed every day and performed numerous rituals. He was in contact with spirits and claimed that many of his abilities and successes were because of their assistance.

The spark of the divine spirit of the universe is also the spirit inside each of us. Ultimately Aikido is a way of finding and

In his youth, Morehei Uyeshiba followed Shinto traditions and beliefs, and in Aikido he was to develop a strong spiritual balance.

developing this inner light, which, at a high level, shines very brightly and is united with the divine light of life.

Morihei wanted Aikido to be a path of peace that people could use not only to transform themselves but also to transform the world. He claimed he wanted Aikido to be a way of creating heaven on earth and of bringing people together in harmony and friendship.

An Aikido Application

In this application the Aikido practitioner responds to the opponent's attack by immediately counter-attacking forward, stepping in with an Atemi.

These movements can be practiced against an imaginary opponent or as a little moving meditation sequence to get an idea of what this style actually feels like.

1. *The opponent steps forward with his left foot and punches straight to the face of the Aikido practitioner with his left fist.*

2. *The Aikido practitioner responds by stepping forward with her right foot, slightly to the side. She simultaneously lifts her hands up straight forward with the fingers pointing forward and the palms facing in toward each other.*

3. The Aikido practitioner strikes straight forward with her left-hand Atemi straight into the left side of the opponent's neck. Her right hand controls the opponent's left arm.

Xiao Jiu Tian

NINE LITTLE HEAVENS

The Nine Little Heavens system is a Daoist internal martial art that is designed to develop and integrate body, mind, and spirit. It is concerned not only with the development of self-defense skills, but also with improving health and increasing longevity.

The system contains empty-hand forms, weapons forms, and Qigong. Its philosophy shows how the individual is a reflection of the wider universe and contains within him or herself all the spiritual elements of the world.

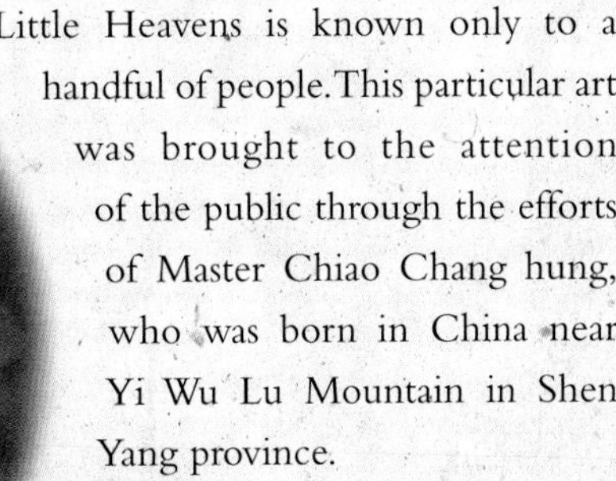

Chiao Chang hung, who has brought this little-known Daoist system to public attention.

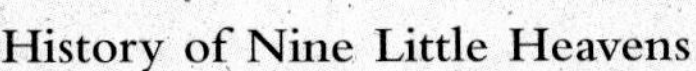

History of Nine Little Heavens

Nine Little Heavens was used by the students of its creator Wu Dao zi to guard the Daoist temples in the Tang Dynasty (A.D. 618-907). The name Nine Little Heavens is in reference to the book of Nine Chamber scriptures written by Huang Di, The Yellow Emperor (2698 - 2598 B.C.).

The system uses movements that are similar to Taijiquan, however it is not nearly as widely practiced - Taijiquan is practiced by millions, but Nine Little Heavens is known only to a handful of people. This particular art was brought to the attention of the public through the efforts of Master Chiao Chang hung, who was born in China near Yi Wu Lu Mountain in Shen Yang province.

In 1898, at the age of 16, Chiao Chang began his training under the Master of the Daoist temple situated on the peak of the Yi Wu Lu Mountain. He went on to become the 33rd-generation teacher of the style, a rare honor, because traditionally the complete system was passed on only to one Daoist disciple in each generation.

The Daoist temple of Yi Wu Lu Mountain, where Chiao Chang hung learned the art of Nine Little Heavens.

THE NINE CHAMBER FIST

The empty-hand set is called the Nine Chamber Fist Form. It is named after the book of Nine Chamber scriptures written by Huang Di, The Yellow Emperor. The practice of this form is relaxed, in order to increase Qi flow and so that martial power will be effective for the self-defense applications. The postures are based on the movements of animals and use locks, throws, kicks, and strikes. It also contains Qigong sets to improve health and develop the spirit.

The movements of the Nine Chamber Fist invigorate energy, which here is concentrated into the two striking fingers of the left hand.

NINE LITTLE HEAVENS WEAPONS

The Nine Little Heavens system also contains weapons forms, which include the Staff and Knife. There is also an interesting Double Sword form, where each of the swords measure over 4 feet (1.3 meters) and on the length of the sword are seven saw teeth near the handle and a further five halfway up the blade. The seven saw teeth correspond to the seven stars of the Big Dipper constellation, which has great significance for Daoist as a source of heavenly Qi that can be accessed during meditation. The five saw teeth correspond to the Five Elements, and training in the Nine Little Heavens system will strengthen the internal organs to which they correspond: Wood - Liver; Fire - Heart; Earth - Spleen; Metal - Lungs; and Water - Kidneys. There are also several sword forms named after different animals: Snake Sword Form, Ape Sword Form, Crane Sword Form, and Dragon Sword Form.

Swords measure over four feet with saw teeth

While this Daoist Nine Little Heavens Weapons Double Sword form is used for self-defense, it also unifies the practitioner with the energies of heaven and earth.

This subtle body map of the inner alchemy from the Ch'ing Dynasty reflects the Daoist theory that the body is a reflection of the universe.

THE BODY AS A SPIRITUAL STRUCTURE

The philosophy of the Nine Little Heavens system is based on the Daoist principle that the body is a reflection of the universe, and within it are all the different aspects that comprise the Dao. The Five Elements relate to the internal organs, and the sixty- four hexagrams of The Yi jing (*Book of Changes*) are contained in the limbs and joints.

The Nine Little Heavens system aims to integrate the mind with the Qi and the body. In its forms and Qigong sets, emphasis is placed on an awareness of the Qi meridian pathways, and also on the ability to encourage Qi to flow through them more strongly.

NINE LITTLE HEAVENS MEDITATION

A practitioner of Nine Little Heavens meditation strives to balance Yin and Yang within him or herself. All the unbalanced aspects of body, mind, and emotions are brought into harmony, and the spirit is strengthened. This balancing of internal energy is made possible by encouraging its flow along the Yin and Yang meridians. This can be achieved through meditation, either standing, sitting, or moving (the moving meditation is the

Achieving Yin/Yang balance through meditation can be reached even while standing.

empty-hand set called The Nine Chamber Fist Form). The purpose of meditation is to balance Yin and Yang within the body and to transform one's Qi into its purest form so we can ascend up to the spiritual world from which we all descend and to which, one day, we will return .

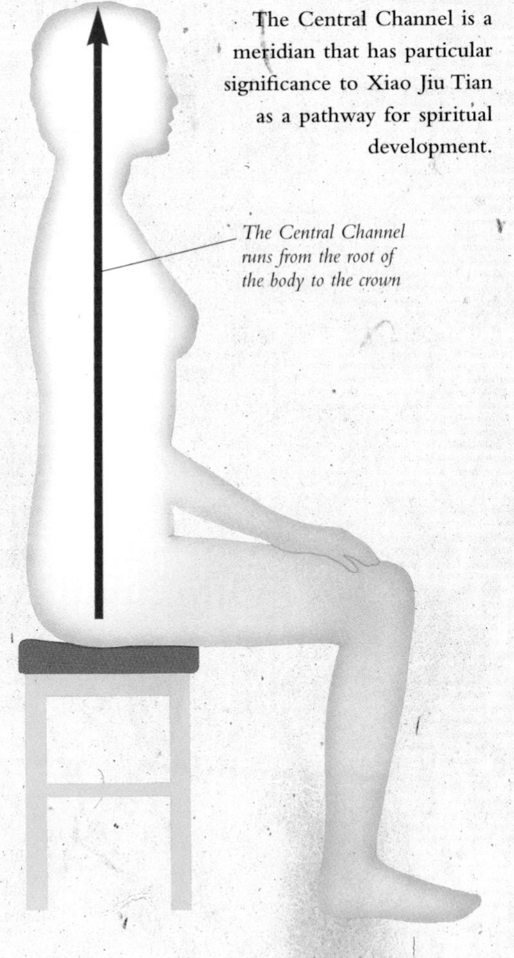
The Central Channel runs from the root of the body to the crown

The Central Channel is a meridian that has particular significance to Xiao Jiu Tian as a pathway for spiritual development.

The Central Channel

In the Nine Little Heavens system, particular emphasis is placed on an awareness of the Central Channel. This is a meridian that runs from the root of the body to the crown. It is possible to activate deep and powerful energy centers in the body that lie along this pathway by leading Qi through it. At the most advanced level we can ascend up this route and then take a spiritual leap out the top of the head.

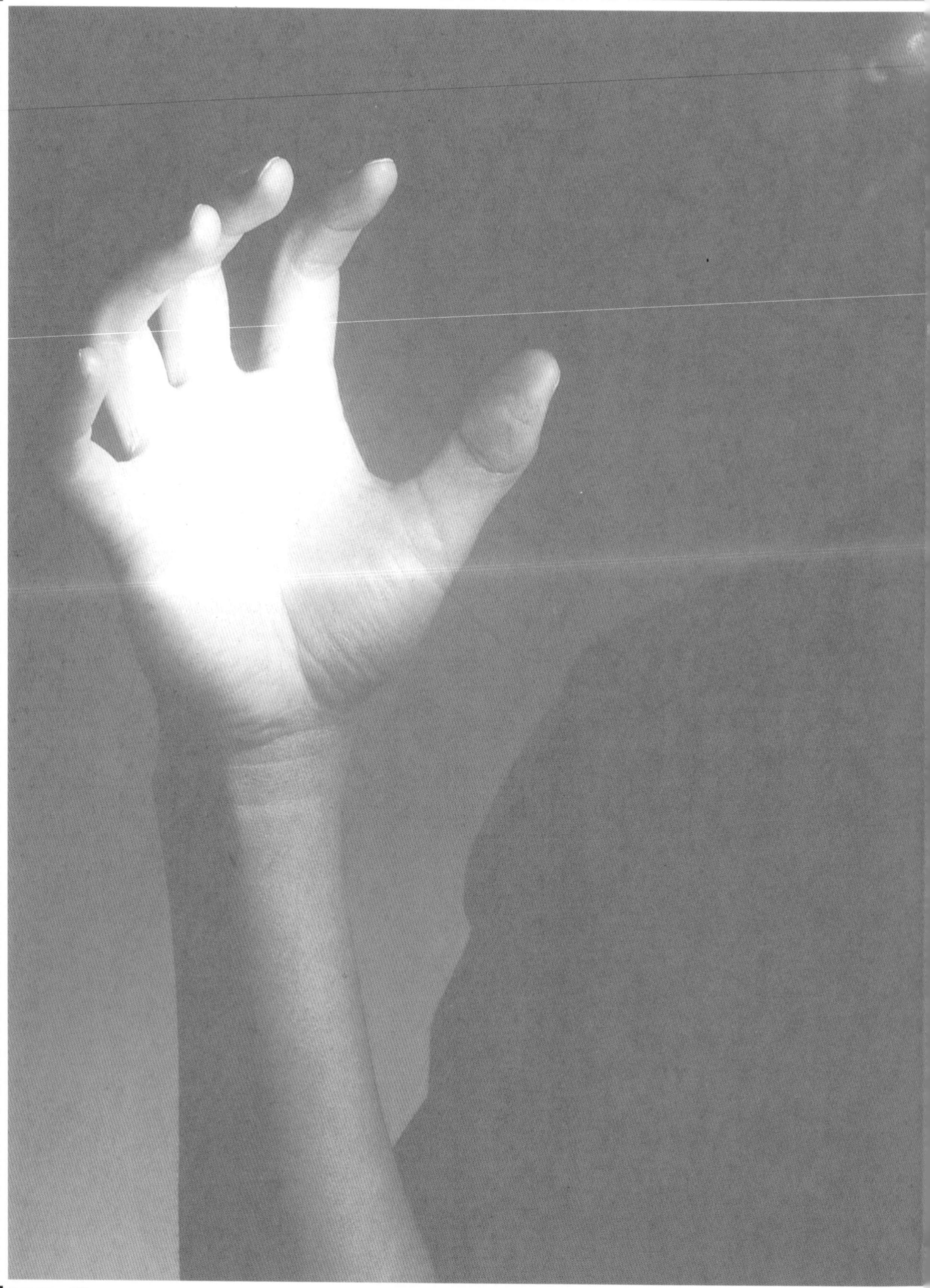

Wu Dang Shan

THE NINE QI DISRUPTION FORMS

THIS FINAL CHAPTER is about the most concealed and hidden of all the internal martial arts, and possibly the one from which the rest derive. The Nine Qi Disruption Forms of the Wudang Shan are about 700 years old and were created by Chang San-feng (see page 44). It was from these forms that Taijiquan evolved, and from which Baguazhang and Xingyiquan were either directly derived or by which they were very heavily influenced.

Master Erle Montaigue, who was privileged to learn the nine forms of Wu Dang Shan.

The Wudang Shan group live on Wudang Mountain in western China. Their current leader, Liang Shih Kan, is over 90 years old. He took over from Dong Kit yung, whose last contact with the outside world was with a reporter from Beijing during 1973. He told the reporter that only family members from the Wudang village received the true art and that outsiders were never taught all of the Nine Qi Disruption Forms, nor their true meaning.

This was the case until very recently, when Master Erle Montaigue received the secrets of all nine of the forms. He is the first westerner to have learned these forms, and it is with his permission that the information contained in this chapter is revealed. (Master Erle Montaigue can be contacted via the Worldwide Web: http://www.ozemail.com.au/~taiji). The forms and their applications can only be learned from him; this chapter is only a brief outline to introduce the reader to some of the basic ideas and concepts of The Nine Qi Disruption Forms of the Wudang Shan.

The mountainous Wudang area of China, whose inhabitants have given rise to many of the soft internal martial arts.

QI DISRUPTION

There are nine empty-hand forms in the Wudang Qi Disruption system. All the forms contain movements similar to Taijiquan, Baguazhang, and Xingyiquan, (or rather Taijiquan, Baguazhang, and Xingyiquan contain movements similar to the Nine Qi Disruption forms.)

The movements contained in the nine forms use the same principles as the other internal martial arts: correct posture, integrated body movement; Rooting; centrifugal and centripetal waist power; and Fa jin.

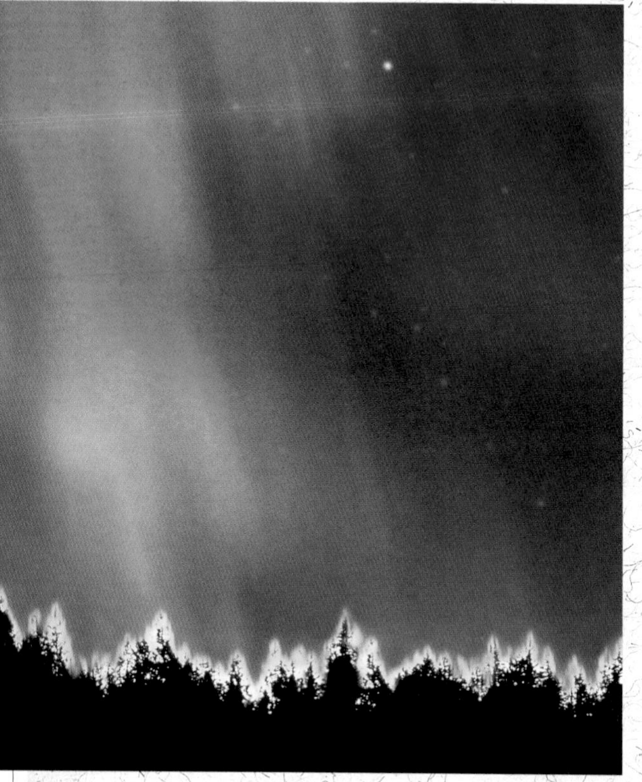

The Northern Lights, which cause computer disruptions at the North Pole similar to the effects of Qi Disruption.

Like the other styles they can be practiced either slowly for health benefits, or explosively for self-defense. However they are performed, the circulation of Qi will be invigorated, and good health and well-being will be assured.

What makes these forms different is that hidden within each form is a special technique called Qi Disruption. This is used in self-defense situations as one is closing with the opponent, when he or she has begun their attack and you move forward to counterattack. There is a moment when you are attacking their attack (for example, striking the forearm of the hand they punched with) before you strike their torso, neck, or head. It is at this point that Qi Disruption is used: the hands are moved in a certain way over specific acupuncture meridians, several inches in front of the opponent's body, thereby causing their Qi to be disrupted in a particular way.

There are nine different Qi Disruption techniques, and each one has a different effect. For example, the Qi can be disrupted in the opponent's arms so that all power is lost and they cannot be used to block your counterattacks. Similarly Qi can be drained from certain areas of the opponent's body, making them very vulnerable to an attack.

The highest level of Qi Disruption is attainable by only a few rare individuals. It is the remarkable and amazing ability of being able to put an opponent to sleep. When we sleep at night the activity and alignment of the Qi in our brains changes. An advanced practitioner of Qi Disruption can intentionally realign the Qi flow in an opponent's head and put them to sleep.

The best way to understand Qi Disruption is to compare it with similar types of electromagnetic field effects. For example, when a very strong magnet is placed near a video or cassette tape,

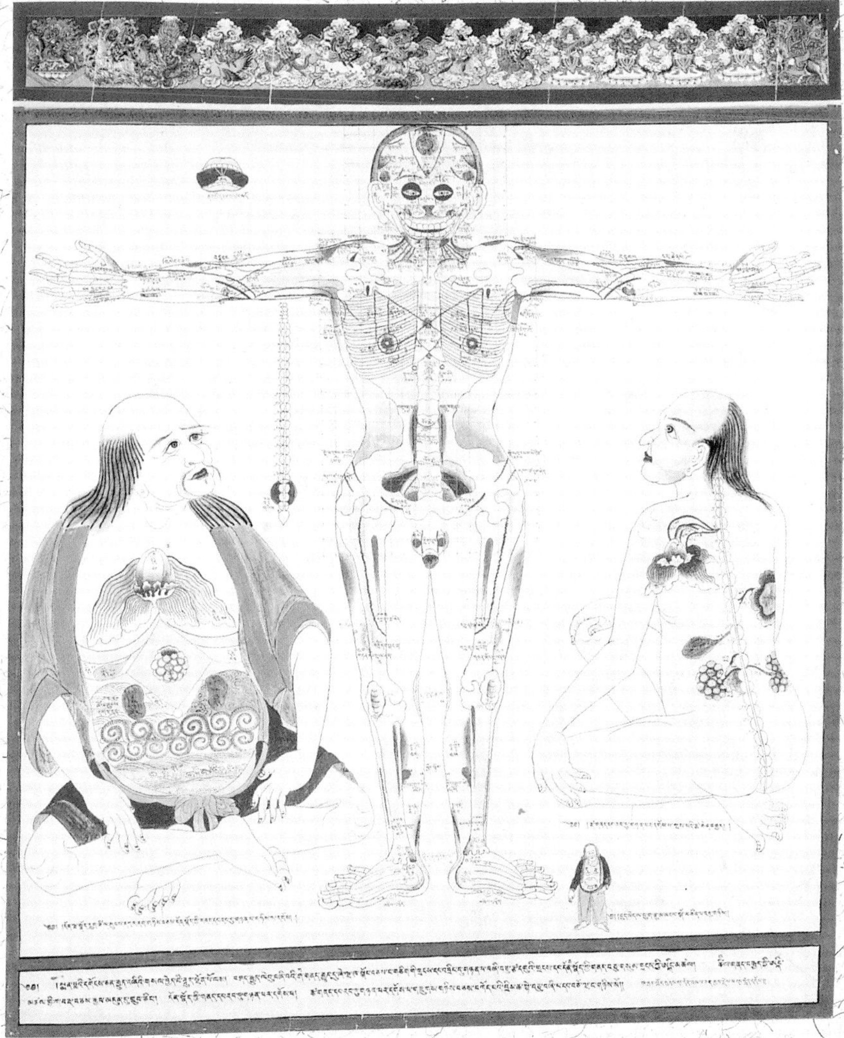

An ancient map showing the organs of the human body, many of which can be disrupted using the nine forms.

they will be ruined. On a larger scale, research scientists based at the North Pole experience computer malfunctions during the activity of the Northern Lights.

It is only possible to disrupt an opponent's Qi if the hands are highly charged and if the body is free from any blocks that would restrict the flow of Qi. Furthermore, the Qi Disruption techniques must be executed as a Fa jin movement in order to work properly. This is why it is not possible for just anyone to practice Qi Disruption. Only those who practice the forms regularly alongside Qigong, and who have mastered all the internal principles, can perform Qi Disruption.

THE NINE QI DISRUPTION FORMS

The following is a list of the Nine Qi Disruption forms, explaining how the body is healed by practicing them and how they can be used to adversely affect the opponent.

The Penetration Form
This is the first of the Qi Disruption forms and is used to penetrate the attacker's defenses. It increases Qi flow through the spleen to strengthen and heal it, and also strengthens the spine and the nervous system and sharpens the reflexes

The Leaping Form
The second Qi Disruption form helps to balance Qi flow between the upper and lower body, as well as strengthening the spleen. It contains a Qi Disruption technique that breaks the Qi flow between the opponent's upper and lower body

The Eight Directions Form
The third Qi Disruption form strengthens the kidneys and improves the reflexes. It contains a Qi Disruption technique that scatters the Qi in the opponent's head

The Spiral Form
The fourth Qi Disruptive form also strengthens the kidneys and the nervous system, and sharpens the reflexes. Baguazhang may have been developed from this form.

The Waving Form
The fifth Qi Disruptive Form strengthens the lungs and can be used to heal many lung ailments. This form increases internal power and contains a Qi disruption technique that drains Qi from the opponent's lungs.

The Closing-up Form
The sixth Qi Disruptive Form strengthens the heart and improves Rooting. It contains techniques that close down the opponent's Qi system.

The One-handed or Water Form
The seventh Qi Disruptive Form strengthens the bladder and improves the flow of Qi from heaven, through the body, into the earth and from the earth, through the body, up to heaven.

The Ground or Earth Form
The eighth Qi Disruptive Form strengthens the stomach and develops Rooting. This form emphasizes the way that movements should flow into one another and encourages Qi to flow more strongly because of its Qigong aspects.

The Wuji Form
The ninth and last Qi Disruptive Form integrates the whole body together and unifies the Qi flow through all the meridians. It balances all the different aspects of Yin and Yang Qi and centers oneself in the Lower Dan Dien.

The nine Qi Disruption forms have two uses; they can be used to heal as well as block an attacker.

THE HEALING ASPECTS OF QI DISRUPTION

The ability to heal another person using a system that involves Qi, such as acupuncture, acupressure massage, or external Qigong healing, depends on the individual's own understanding of and ability to manipulate Qi.

If we can generate a great amount of Qi and circulate it around the body, and if we can open up to allow Qi from heaven and earth to flow through us, then we will be more successful when we try to heal others.

Fa jin and Qi Disruption are ways of developing the ability to generate Qi and emit it from the body into another person. For self-defense these movements are done explosively and with an aggressive intention. During healing Qi is emitted with much more gentle movements and with a positive healing intention.

The principle is the same for both applications, and this is why the Qi Disruption forms of the Wudang Shan, and all the other internal martial arts covered in this book, are of such great benefit. Through regular daily practice, practioners can not only develop good self-defense skills, but can also increase their Qi energy and their creative potential, improve their physical health and longevity, balance their mind and emotions, and develop a clear, strong spirit.

Healing, using various techniques connected with Qi flow, uses positive energies.

INDEX

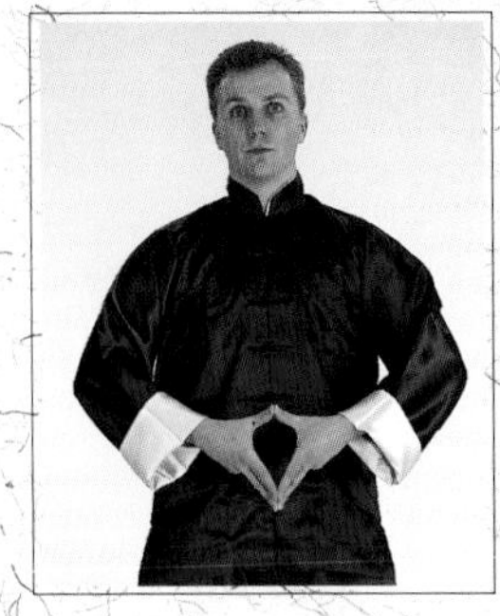

ABOUT THE AUTHOR

Paul Brecher has over 20 years' experience in the martial arts and is a Senior Instructor of The World Taijiquan (Tai Chi) Boxing Association. He has written numerous articles for magazines and given many Taijiquan demonstrations on television. His book *The Principles of Tai Chi* (Thorsons, 1997) contains information about Tai Chi not previously revealed to the public and has become "the" reference work for all serious students of the art.

In his London classes he teaches:

Yang Lu Chan's Old Yang Style
  Taijiquan Long Form
The Old Yang Style Taijiquan San Sau
  Two-Person Fighting Form
The Old Yang Style Taijiquan Pauchui
  Cannon Fist Form
Taijiquan Weapons Forms: Double Saber,
  Staff, and Walking Stick

He also teaches:

Pushing hands, Da Lu, and Taijiquan
  Lung Har Chuan
Three Circle Qigong, The Small Circulation,
  and Large Circulation of Qi
Iron Shirt and Iron Palm Qigong
The Twelve Taijiquan Dimmak Palms

In addition to his involvement in the martial arts, he is also a practitioner of Traditional Chinese Medicine.

Paul Brecher BA MAcS MPCHM (Bachelor of Arts, Member Of The Acupuncture Society, and Member Practitioner of Chinese Herbal Medicine) can be contacted at the following address:
Paul Brecher
PO Box 13219
London
NW11 7WS
England
UK
http://www.taiji.net

List of Sources

Brecher, Paul, *Principles of Tai Chi*
(Thorsons, UK, 1997)
Liang, Yang and Wu, *Baguazhang*,
(YMMA Publications, USA, 1994)
Liang and Yang, *Hsing Yi Chuan*,
(YMMA Publications, Hong Kong, 1990)
Stevens, John, *Abundant Peace*,
(Shambhala, USA, 1987)

The publishers wish to thank the following for use of pictures:

AKG photo, Axiom Photographic Agency, Biofotos, Colour Library Images, Eye Ubiquitous, Sally & Richard Greenhill, Horizon, Hutchison Library, The Image Bank, The Stock Market, Tibet Image Bank, John Walmsley.